FOUR
SHORT PLAYS

BY MARK MEDOFF

THE FROEGLE DICTUM
DOING A GOOD ONE FOR THE RED MAN
THE ULTIMATE GRAMMAR OF LIFE
THE WAR ON TATEM

★

★

DRAMATISTS
PLAY SERVICE
INC.

CONTENTS

4

THE FROEGLE DICTUM

A PLAY IN ONE ACT
BY MARK MEDOFF

CHARACTERS

RONALD NABORS

MANDY

AL SIMON

HARRIET BEADLING

THE FROEGLE DICTUM

A one room apartment with kitchenette Up Center. Each half of the apartment has a bed and an easy chair, however, there is a great difference between the two sides. The Left side is very bookish and domesticated looking— curtains at the window, everything in its place. The other side is a shambles, marked most noticeably by broken destruction devices—guns, rifles, knives, swords, empty medicine bottles. The kitchenette is similarly divided, the one side scrubbed and ordered, the other piled with dirty dishes, utensils, pans and pots. The front door is in the Left half, the walk-in closet/bathroom door in the Right half.

Nabors and Mandy occupy the clean half. Nabors, 21, a fat young man in jacket and tie, smoking a pipe, sits in his easy chair with a book. Mandy, 19, a beautiful, doll-like creature, sits on the bed in a flowing nightgown, brushing her hair, and though her hair is long to begin with, she brushes it as if it were considerably longer than it is. There is about them a mannequin quality, they are vaguely mechanical and unable to look directly at whomever they speak to. Nabors underlines the book he reads with a felt pen, grunting in agreement with the content.

MANDY. (*Brushing her hair, counting the strokes in a whisper.*) Four thousand nine hundred and seventy-two, four thousand nine hundred and seventy-three, four thousand nine hundred and seventy-four— (*She continues counting to herself. The front door opens and Al enters. He is perhaps just slightly older than Nabors and Mandy. He is carrying a paper sack with a noose in it. He is sloppily dressed, disheveled, and has a suicidal look about him. He glances obviously at Mandy as he enters. Neither Nabors nor Mandy looks at him.*)
NABORS. Shoes off, Al.
AL. They're clean.

NABORS. Shoes off, Al. (*Al retreats to the doorway, showing no irritation, no emotion at all particularly, except a certain low key single-mindedness which has to do with his continuing efforts to kill himself. He removes his shoes; his socks are stiff looking and soiled.*) Thank you, Al.

MANDY. Hi, Al. Look—I'm brushing my hair.

AL. (*Crossing to his side of the apartment.*) Uhm.

MANDY. Geez, Al, the b.o.'s a little stronger than usual today, wouldn't ya say? I would. I'd say it's a little stronger than usual today. Wouldn't you, Ronny? Say that the b.o.—

NABORS. According to my records, Al, it's been twenty-two days since you last bathed. About time for a shower, isn't it? (*Al pays no attention to Nabors, though he might take a couple of surreptitious glances at Mandy to see if she's looking at what he's doing—which she isn't. He has thrown off his dirty fatigue jacket. He removes the noose from the sack and looks for something to throw the end over; finds nothing.*)

AL. Nabors, co'mere.

NABORS. (*Looking up for the first time.*) Ah—another suicide attempt, is it, Al?

AL. Yeah.

NABORS. It'll never work, Al.

AL. Can't miss. Co'mere.

NABORS. Can I handle my end from our side? I just got these slacks back from the cleaners.

AL. Over here.

NABORS. How about taking a shower first, Al? You don't want to go out smelling like dead fish, do you?

AL. Yeah. Ya comin or not? I haven't got all day.

NABORS. Okay, Al, okay. Don't get your bowels in an uproar.

MANDY. (*Gayly.*) It smells like he already has. (*Al looks at Mandy who smiles plastically in his direction. His eyes linger on her.*)

AL. I'll be dead in a minute and you can have the stink outta here inside an hour. (*But she has returned to her brushing and stroke-counting. Nabors meanwhile has put on an overcoat and is getting into a pair of workman's gloves and a gas mask. Lastly, he puts on a pair of high-top, buckle galoshes which he doesn't buckle. He tip-toes into Al's half of the apartment.*) Get up there and hold this. (*Nabors gets up on the bed with his book in one hand, opened,* and the end of the noose in the other. *Al slips the noose over his head and hands Nabors the end, then gets up on the bed with Nabors.*)

NABORS. (*During the foregoing.*) I'm reading Arnold Froegle this afternoon, Al.

AL. Uhm.

NABORS. And I'm afraid what Froegle boils down to is this: Cruelty— (*Then he sings to the tune of "Harrigan."*) C-R-U-E-L-T-Y-Y spells cruelty cruelty . . .

AL. Hold your end up, Nabors. . . . Higher.

NABORS. That *cruelty*, Al, is the single act most common to God and Man. And he asks, Al, can that be? Can that *be?*, he asks. (*Al jumps. The rope is too loose in the distance between him and Nabors.*)

AL. Christ.

NABORS. He asks, Can we *permit* that to be?

AL. Ya gotta hold your end up *higher*, Nabors.

NABORS. And as our leading positivist philosopher, Al, he answers a resounding—

AL. Hold it tight, Nabors. Ya gotta hold it tight enough so that when I jump there's no slack and it breaks my neck.

NABORS. Give it up, Al. Look at all this junk.

AL. This'll work if you do what you're supposed to.

NABORS. Switch to Froegle, Al. He gives us ten easy steps to a positive life, beginning with an embracing of— (*Al has climbed back up on the bed, drawn the line tight in Nabors' hand and raised Nabors' arm as high as it will go.*)

AL. So long, Nabors. Say g'bye to Froegle for me.

NABORS. See you in a minute, Al.

AL. This is it. Keep any of my shit ya want.

NABORS. Not likely.

AL. So long, Mandy . . . Mandy . . .

MANDY. Oh!—so long, Al.

AL. I'm killin myself.

MANDY. It won't be the same without you.

AL. Whudduya mean?

MANDY. I don't know. (*She looks away and goes on with her hair. Al looks lingeringly at her a moment, then jumps. The noose breaks.*)

AL. Christ. What kinda rope *is* this?

NABORS. Looks like somebody cut through it. It's no good, Al. Give it up.

AL. Never. (*Al picks up a broken sword—handle and a foot or so of steel. He drives it at his belly. The sword breaks.*) Christ. (*He throws himself on the bed. Nabors tip-toes back to his side, removes the coat, gloves, galoshes, and gas mask, sits back down in his easy chair to read and smoke his pipe.*)

MANDY. Ronny! Where have you been? I missed you.

NABORS. Al just tried to hang himself.

MANDY. Oh! —howd it go?

NABORS. Good for Froegle, bad for Al.

MANDY. Oh, that's too bad. (*Calling to Al.*) That's too bad, Al.

AL. Yeah. (*Then snapping up and screaming at her.*) A lot you care. (*Neither she nor Nabors seems to hear him. Nabors reads, she brushes. Al leaps up and goes to the refrigerator, he takes out a very moldy sandwich.*) How long's this baloney sandwich been in here?

MANDY. (*Without looking at him.*) Your baloney or ours?

AL. Mine. Whuddo I want with yours?

MANDY. Uh . . . seven months and three days. (*Al gobbles up the sandwich, standing at the demarcation between the two halves of the apartment, directly across from Mandy, who pays him not the slightest heed. He flops on the bed.*)

AL. When I start screaming, don't call an ambulance or there's gonna be a scene.

MANDY. We won't.

AL. I just poisoned myself.

MANDY. Eww!

AL. It was a free choice.

NABORS. To get back to what I was saying, Al: All right, we cannot change God, as Froegle points out, but Man, Al: Man! (*Nabors delivers a little laugh, full of hope for "Man," accompanied by a hopefully clenched fist and jaw.*)

MANDY. Five thousand! Everybody! Look at my hair!

NABORS. And, Al . . . Al, let me begin with you—yes yes— why not with you, Al?

AL. I think I'm starting to go.

MANDY. You don't want to die, Al. Oh surely not.

AL. Whudduyou care?

MANDY. You know what all Al needs is, Ronny? (*Nabors is into*

10

his book and pipe.) Ronny? (*Nothing, so toward Al.*) You know what all Al needs is, Al?

NABORS. Froegle's first step, Al, on the trail to a road of positive living is Cleanliness. Bodily cleanliness. (*Takes a deep breath.*)

AL. Here it comes. (*He recoils against a stomach spasm.*)

MANDY. A girlfriend, Al, to live on your side like I live on Ronny's is all you needs—need; is all you *need*. . . . Al? . . . Ronny?

AL. That was a good one. That felt good. I think the baloney's gonna do the trick.

MANDY. Don't you agree, Ronny? . . . Al? (*A knock at the door.*) Oh goody—company, and look at my hair, ready just in time. (*She arranges her nightgown around her, tosses her hair.*) Come in. (*Harriet Beadling enters—an unattractive girl who trips as she enters and then stands unsurely in the doorway.*) Oh! Harriet! You scared me.

HARRIET. Oh—well, I'm sorry, I—

MANDY. Geez, who put your make-up on?

HARRIET. I did.

MANDY. God.

HARRIET. Does it look—

MANDY. (*With a touch of childish anger.*) You *scared* me.

HARRIET. I'm sorry, I—

MANDY. Phew! Don't ever do that *again*. What do you want?

HARRIET. Well, you said to come to this address, so I came. (*Harriet holds out a slip of paper.*)

MANDY. (*Looking across space at the slip of paper a moment.*) I know.

HARRIET. Should I come in or what?

MANDY. Uhm . . .

HARRIET. What did you want me to come for?

MANDY. Uhm . . . Oh!—I have somebody I want you to meet.

HARRIET. Why me?

MANDY. What?

HARRIET. Why me?

MANDY. What?

HARRIET. I said, Why *me*?

MANDY. Oh! . . . Well . . . Oh yeah! Wouldn't you like to meet somebod, ? You looked like a person that would like to meet

11

somebody. A boy? A man, I mean. A man. Wouldn't you like to meet a man of my acquaintance?

HARRIET. I . . . Well I mean . . . who? Sure—I guess—who?

MANDY. What?

HARRIET. Who *is* he?

MANDY. Uhm . . . Oh yeah! He's my boyfriend Ronald Nabors' roommate, Al. (*Mandy indicates Nabors in the above after first mistakenly indicating Al. Then when she has that straight, she indicates Al on "Al."*) He just came back from the war a few short months ago. He was a soldier. He knows a lot about war. Ask him about war if you want to know why my boyfriend Ronald Nabors is all the time saying how we have to get out of . . . whachacallit—or else. Al—you'll like him.

HARRIET. Oh . . . Al.

MANDY. (*Can't remember what to do next.*) Uhm . . Oh yeah! Okay: introductions, everybody! (*Neither Al nor Nabors pays any attention. Al continues to die and Nabors reads.*) Uhm . . . Harriet Berman—

HARRIET. Beadling.

MANDY. —Beadling, this is Ronald my boyfriend Nabors. My boyfriend, I mean, Ronald—Ronny—Ron Newland—

NABORS. Nabors.

MANDY. Nabors, I mean. Ronald—Ron, I mean, meet Harriet Berman—

HARRIET. Beadling.

MANDY. —Beadling.

NABORS. Hello.

HARRIET. Hello.

NABORS. (*With the same intonation as the first, slightly over-lapping her.*) Hello.

MANDY. (*Indicating Al.*) And this . . . (*She does an egregiously obsequious trumpet flourish on her hair brush—buh duh dub deet doo doot, then.*) . . . this is the Famous Alan—

NABORS. Al.

MANDY. —Al . . . Simons.

NABORS. Simon.

MANDY. —Simon—Ronald's—Ronny's—Ron's and mine's roommate.

NABORS. Mine.

12

MANDY. Ron and mine roommate.

NABORS. Ron's and mine roommate.

MANDY. Ron's and mine roommate.

HARRIET. (*To Al, who does not look or respond in the least.*) Hello.

NABORS. What do you mean by the "famous" Al, Mandy? The "famous" Al. I'm afraid I don't get that.

MANDY. (*Aside to Nabors, flatting a hand to the side of her mouth, obviously cutting out nobody.*) I'm just trying to make Al sound like hot spit, Ronny.

NABORS. No no no, mustn't do. No no no. You mustn't create any added pressures for Al by—

MANDY. (*Going to the division line but not crossing.*) Aren't you famous, Al?

AL. Uh?

MANDY. I mean, aren't you the famous Al, Al?

AL. (*Through a stomach spasm.*) Yeah. I'm famous.

MANDY. See?

AL. (*Through a stomach spasm, to Harriet.*) I'm the famous Al. (*Looking at her for the first time.*) Who the hell are you?

HARRIET. How do you do, the famous Al, I'm—

AL. How do I do what?

HARRIET. (*Pause.*) Well, for instance, how do you do what you're doing now?

AL. Baloney sandwich.

HARRIET. Oh.

MANDY. (*Gayly.*) Al's committing suicide.

HARRIET. Oh . . . How come?

MANDY. I don't know. He's been doing it a couple of times a day for months. Go figure people out.

NABORS. What's Al famous for, Mandy; let's get that straight before we fly off into the hinterland.

MANDY. Uhm . . .

NABORS. What are you famous for, Al?

AL. (*Through a heavy spasm.*) In Saigon once . . . Augh! . . . I blew my nose on a hooker's head. Augh!—that was a good one. I think I'm gonna buy the deep six on the next one. So long, Mandy.

MANDY. Al, Harriet has Abnormal Psych with me.

AL. (*Through a spasm.*) I suppose I'm supposed to be pretty

13

tickled by that, huh; when I'm lyin here dyin from a baloney sandwich.

HARRIET. It's a good course. I'm learning a lot.

AL. God, that's great.

HARRIET. See how fun Al is, Harriet.

AL. I thought that last one was gonna do the job. But here I am.

NABORS. (*Deep in his book, with exuberance.*) Oh Al oh Al— life— (*Cuts himself off and holds a big plastic smile several moments before returning into his book.*)

HARRIET. How come you're trying to kill yourself?

AL. Don't wanna live.

HARRIET. How come?

AL. Don't like it.

MANDY. (*And aside to Al with one hand.*) Live for Harriet, Al. (*And aside to Harriet with the other hand.*) Go to him, Harriet, you dope.

HARRIET. (*Smiling unsurely, then moving hesitantly toward Al's half.*) Can I do anything for you?

AL. (*Through a spasm.*) Yeah . . . ya got any poison on ya? I think I'm gonna need a chaser on this baloney.

MANDY. Al, aren't you gonna invite Harriet to sit down and have a beer of her choice?

AL. Uh-uh.

MANDY. There, Harriet, sit down in Al's chair.

AL. Don't try it.

MANDY. What brand of beer do you enjoy?

AL. I'm outta beer.

MANDY. *We're* not. (*Goes to refrigerator.*) Here, Harriet, we have this brand. Help yourself to this one.

NABORS. Just a second there, Mandy. (*Takes notepad from his jacket.*) I'm going to have to ask you to sign an IOU on this, Al. (*Scribbles note, passes it and pen to Harriet.*) Pass these on to Al, will you. Sign at the bottom, Al. (*Al signs at the bottom and tosses the pad and pen at Harriet, who picks them up and passes them back to Nabors.*) Enjoy your beer, Harriet.

HARRIET. I don't drink beer.

NABORS. That's too bad. We went to some trouble there.

AL. Lemme have it. Who knows what kinda chemical reaction I can work up with beer and poison baloney. (*Mandy passes the beer to Harriet who passes it to Al.*)

14

MANDY. Look, Al, look how much of a help Harriet is already. You just come right in and start helping away, don't you, Harriet. God. Would you like some cocoa?

HARRIET. All right.

MANDY. With a big marshmallow that you can make go squish squish?

HARRIET. Uh-huh.

NABORS. We don't have any cocoa.

MANDY. We don't have any cocoa, Harriet.

HARRIET. Oh—that's okay.

MANDY. Phew! Thanks—that was a close one. (*To Nabors.*) That was a close one, huh Ronny? (*To Harriet.*) Got some fresh parsley.

HARRIET. Oh well—

MANDY. Ronny's making linguine with clam sauce for our dinner. The clams are canned, but oh you parsley. Ronny does all our cooking. He's a magician around the stove, I'm tellin ya. What are you and Harriet having for dinner, Al?

AL. (*Spasm.*) Augh!

HARRIET. (*Creeping toward Al.*) Would you like me to make you something to eat?

AL. Augh!

MANDY. Al has some bouillon cubes on his side of the frig. I don't know if they're beef or chicken, but they've only been in there about five months. Should Harriet make you some bouillon, Al?

AL. (*Through clenched teeth, result of the last spasm.*) Get her outta here!

MANDY. Al's really a lot of fun, Harriet, once you get to know him. Don't give up on him yet, okay?

HARRIET. No. I won't.

MANDY. Oh!—that's good news. Harriet's not going to give up on Al yet, Ronny. (*Back to Harriet.*) Most of them give up by the second or third Get out!, Harriet. You've got a lot of gumption, haven't you?

HARRIET. Al, should I make you a nice cup of hot bouillon?

NABORS. Not hot, I'm afraid. Al's two burners have been shut down. Didn't pay his gas bill. Have to be cold bouillon.

HARRIET. Surely I can use one of your burners, then, to make—

15

MANDY. Of course you can. She can use one of our burners, can't she, Ronny?

NABORS. Nope, fraid not.

MANDY. I'm afraid you can't use one of our burners, Harriet.

NABORS. I'm going to be into some clam sauce and linguine here before you know it, and I'm not coming to a pre-heated burner with fresh parsley.

HARRIET. Would you like some cold bouillon, Al?

NABORS. Do you know what I think, Harriet?

HARRIET. Uhm . . . no I don't think I do—

NABORS. (*Over her, completely ignoring whatever she might have said.*) When a new person sits down here with us, I always like to tell him or her what I think about at least one of the many things that I think something about. Would you care to pick a topic or shall I just dive in somewhere—

HARRIET. Oh well, if it's all the same—

NABORS. (*Over her.*) Why don't I tell you what I think about why Al continually manages to fail in his efforts to commit suicide?

HARRIET. Oh that's all right; I'm taking Abnormal Psych, I'd rather figure it out my—

NABORS. I should preface my remarks by noting that Al has no purpose in life; he has no—

AL. For chrissake, Nabors, look at yourself, will ya. (*To Harriet.*) Will you look at who's talkin.

NABORS. Typical Simon ploy, Harriet. Turning the subject on an object, thereby objectifying the subject and subjectifying the object. Rusty old existentialist gambit, Al. Grow up philosophically, will you. Here, take a look at Froegle if you want to invest in—

AL. Why don't ya go on a diet or somethin, ya cretin.

NABORS. I have a gland problem, Al, and you know it. Is that fun, to pick on a person's gland problem? To Al, Harriet, it's quite some fun, you see, to pick on a fat person's gland problem. Hey, lookit the kid with the gland problem—let's go give it to him about this malaise about which he is powerless to do anything. Hey you, fat kid with the gland problem—

AL. Goddamnit, you're ruinin the baloney, Nabors! Go join the army or somethin, will ya!

NABORS. I'm 4-F, Al, and you know it. I'm never going to make a personal appearance at the war. But as you *well* know, Al, I'm fighting it here with all the heart I have.

AL. Bullshit—

NABORS. Which is a lot more than you've done since you got back—

AL. Bull. Shit.

NABORS. Take a lesson in positive moral commitment from Froegle—

AL. Shit of the bull, Nabors.

MANDY. You know what Al needs a lot more than Froegle, Ronny? (*Nothing.*) Harriet? (*Nothing.*) Al?

AL. Christ, there goes the baloney.

MANDY. A girl to live with in his half of the apartment like I live in Ronny's. (*Al and Nabors stare at each other. Harriet looks from Mandy to Al.*) Everybody! I'm going to do my toenails! (*Mandy takes up her pedicure set from the bed stand and goes to work. Al leaps up and heads for the stove. He throws the oven open, flips the dial and sticks his head in. Nabors leaps up, rushes over, pulls Al out, and turns off the gas.*)

NABORS. There are other people living here, Al, who aren't in the mood for asphyxiation—to say nothing of the fact that the oven belongs to us. (*Al rips back to the bed, grabs up the beer can, empties the remaining beer on the floor, crunches the can in half and madly bends it back and forth until it halves. He takes a jagged half and slashes at his wrist. No blood.*) Give it up, Al. (*Al throws the beer can half into Nabors and Mandy's half and collapses back on the bed.*) Hey! —keep that junk on your side! Get that beer can, Mandy, and throw it back on Al the Slob's side.

MANDY. I'm doing my toenails. *You're* in charge of cleaning anyway, Ronny. No fair shirking.

NABORS. You're a real slob, Al. (*Nabors throws an apron on and lumbers after the beer can half.*) Don't be a litterbug over here, Al, I won't have it. (*Nabors kicks the beer can half back to Al's side, takes off the apron, and sits back down to read.*)

HARRIET. (*To Al.*) Can I do something for you? (*No response.*) You know what I do when I get depressed? (*Al jams the pillow over his head.*) I draw treasure maps on white bond paper with crayons and then I make the maps look real old by burning them here and there on an electric stove. (*Al looks out at her with open-mouthed disdain.*) To make them look like parchment. (*Al stares at her. Harriet nods to assure him this is good therapy. Al gets back under the pillow.*)

17

NABORS. Oh this Froegle! Yes yes! *Here* is a man, Al, who knows the *value* of life.

HARRIET. Hey, Al—lookit what I can do. Can you do this? (*She makes a "funny" face. Al looks out from under the pillow.*)

AL. Oh man, hey, don't do that. Wow. Hey, that's really awful.

HARRIET. (*Breaking the face.*) I know it, but it's just something I feel helplessly compelled to do at various times. Look at this one that's sweeping like some kind of juggernaut over my fantastically malleable face. (*She makes another "funny" face.*) Can you do this one?

AL. Oh *Christ!*

HARRIET. (*Breaking the face and saying deadly seriously.*) You try it or I'll boot you right in the chops. (*Then a sudden smile.*) Look. (*She makes the face again, says through it.*) Can you do this?

AL. No, but I can do this. (*Maniacally he sits up and begins to choke himself. His eyes bulge and his breath rasps in his throat and he lives. He throws his hands off and collapses back onto the pillow.*) You got a bottle of sleeping pills maybe?

HARRIET. Uh-uh.

AL. How bout a bottle of anything?

HARRIET. Vitamins.

AL. Hey, Nabors, can a bottle of vitamins kill ya?

NABORS. Eh?

AL. *Vitamins*—a bottle of 'em!—Can they *kill* ya?

NABORS. Certainly not. Vitamins make you live *longer.*

AL. Christ, I'm glad I found out before it was too early.

NABORS. Hmm?

AL. Skip it!

NABORS. Al, you've got to delve into Froegle's negation of Schopenhauer's nihilism.

MANDY. Look, everybody, five toes done! (*Al yanks the blanket haphazardly over himself and covers his head with the pillow.*)

HARRIET. I'm going to clean up here a little, Al. Do you mind?

AL. Yeah.

HARRIET. Well I'm going to anyway. (*She goes to the kitchenette and picks up a nice big, clean kitchen wastebasket from Nabors' and Mandy's side.*)

NABORS. That's our trash receptacle, Harriet.

HARRIET. Oh—well I'm just going to—

NABORS. There's Al's. (*He points to an overflowing paper bag on*

Al's side of the kitchenette. Harriet indicates it, smiles sheepishly at Nabors who watches her like a hawk. She looks about, sights an empty duffel bag. She looks at Nabors who nods and returns to his book. She begins to load the duffel bag with the junk littering Al's side.)

HARRIET. Can I ask you something, Al?

AL. Uh-uh.

HARRIET. I mean here's something I really wonder about and you, being a . . . you know . . . you could I bet very handily answer it. I mean, are we . . . do you think we're really justified in being in the war? I mean . . . are we really justified in being there . . . or is it . . . *(Her voice trails off as she finds Al staring at her blankly.)* Oh. Did I . . . Did something awful happen to you or . . . *(Her voice trails off again and he disappears under the pillow. She holds a moment.)* You're definitely one of the best conversationalists I've run into in a long time. It's no wonder I've stayed longer than any of the others. You're a fascinating person. *(Al leaps up, grabs the duffel bag, and dumps what she's collected back on the floor.)*

AL. Who asked ya to stay?

HARRIET. No one.

AL. That's right.

HARRIET. I know it.

AL. So then, get out why don't ya! *(He drops into the chair, grabbing the blanket and covering himself.)*

HARRIET. Uh-uh. You're crying for help—so I'm going to help you.

AL. Oh that's excellent. No joke. Why don't you and Nabors form a partnership? I think the two of ya would make a great team. The Madame Curie and Abraham Lincoln of the altruism field.

HARRIET. *(Making his bed, minus the blanket.)* He's a very intelligent person, isn't he—Ronald Nabors? I mean, would you say he's pretty well got his finger on the pulse of our generation?

AL. Nabors has his head up the ass of our generation and what's happened is the sphincter muscle's frozen shut and he can't get it out.

HARRIET. *(Sardonically, smiling.)* I see.

AL. *(Jumping up and tearing the bed apart.)* Who told ya to make the bed? *(She stares at him, unmoving.)* Huh?

HARRIET. You'd feel better if things were neat. (*Al grabs up a plastic bag and pulls it over his head. He tries to suffocate himself. He breathes deeply several times.*) There's a hole in it. (*Al rips the bag off, sticks his fingers through the hole, tears the bag up and throws the pieces to the floor.*)

NABORS. Give it up, Al. It's no good. (*Harriet is on the opposite side of the bed from Al. He jumps on the bed and grabs her by the collar.*)

AL. (*Livid, but straining to sound controlled.*) Look, uh, Harriet . . . I don't wanna have a relationship with you. Ya know what I mean?—

HARRIET. Oh yes, I think I know what you mean, but what you just said isn't what you mean—

AL. So I'll just say so long and thanks for droppin by and now get out.

HARRIET. You're wrinkling.

MANDY. Ten toes! On to fingernails! (*Al drops on the bed and covers himself with the blanket and pillow. Nabors gets up and goes to Mandy, taking the book with him.*)

NABORS. How about a yummy before dinner, Mandy-pandy?

MANDY. Oh goodey! —but watch my toes, they're not dry. (*Nabors gets fully clothed into bed on top of Mandy, managing to hold the book out where he can still read it. He pulls the bedspread up so that they're almost completely covered. They begin to move together in metronomic sync.*) Oh Ronald Nabors! My b-body, my b-body! (*Al slowly comes out from under the pillow, staring with open envy at Nabors on top of Mandy. Harriet looks from Al to Nabors and Mandy and back to Al, her awareness of Al, it would seem, somewhat sharpened. The lights begin to fade as this action begins until there is semi-darkness.*)

HARRIET. Al . . . ? Can I . . . can I make you something to eat? . . . You want to go out for something? . . . Al? . . . You should eat something.

MANDY. Oooooooh, Ronald Naaaaabors!

HARRIET. What say we go out for a pizza? . . . I'll pay. Whadduya say? . . . Al . . . ?

MANDY. Here it comes! Here it comes! Aaaaaaaaaaaaah! . . . Oooh—there it goes. (*Nabors lumber-leaps out of bed, slams his book shut, and heads for the refrigerator.*)

NABORS. *On to clam sauce!*

(*Blackout. Lights up: the next morning. Al is asleep in the disheveled heap of his bed. Nabors and Mandy are asleep side by side— Mandy closer to center—both on their backs, both with their hands folded on their chests, Mandy is wearing a plastic smile, Nabors a plastic frown. Nabors is covered by a blanket of open books. A clean spaghetti pot and sauce pan, two plates, two wine glasses, some utensils sparkle in a drain rack on their side of the kitchenette. Al's side of the apartment is neat as a pin, except for the area he occupies. The garbage bag is gone, the duffel bag is filled with the débris from the floor and stands in a corner. Harriet comes away fom the kitchen counter with breakfast for Al, complete with a flower in a glass. She sets the tray down and shakes Al gently. Al stirs, peeks out from under the pillow.*)

HARRIET. Good morning, Al.
AL. Christ, what stinks?
HARRIET. Cleanliness and breakfast. (*He sits up with a start, looks around, groans, collapses back.*)
AL. I thought you left last night.
HARRIET. I did.
AL. Then what're ya *doin* here?
HARRIET. I came back last night after I left.
AL. *Why?*
HARRIET. Oh, I just went to buy groceries. (*Picks up tray.*) Here, sit up. I made breakfast for us. I made what you like: Uhm, a nice aluminum bowl chock full of *Gravy Train,* see? —it makes its own gravy, look—and here are several egg flavored Pooch bisquits. (*Al jolts up to look.*) Only kidding. Can't you recognize a joke when you hear one? Eggs and bacon and coffee. (*Al retches over the other side of the bed.*) You can have mine even, if you want. Mandy told me that's what they have for breakfast and that you always lay over here and drool all over yourself, so I thought—
AL. Yeah, well Mandy's a *moron.*
HARRIET. She is not a moron—
AL. She's a moron! Get that gruel away from me before I puke—
HARRIET. You don't have to say things like that. I'm not impressed.
AL. I'm really gonna go outta my way to impress you, right?—
HARRIET. It so happens that after you and Ronald Nabors went to sleep last night, Mandy helped me put the food away and we had

21

a very nice conversation about you. She happens to be very fond of you.

AL. Who is?

HARRIET. (*Pointing at Mandy.*) Mandy. Now eat!

AL. I don't wanna eat. You eat!

HARRIET. All right, I will. But you'll be sorry when you come down with heart disease or something from not eating properly.

AL. I'd pay *money* for heart disease! (*Pause, staring at her.*) Whudduya mean, she's *fond* of me?

HARRIET. (*Eating.*) She's just very fond of you.

AL. I bet. The only time she even comes over on my side of the apartment is when she has to go to the toilet, and then Nabors has to get into his evacuation gear and carry her so she doesn't have to step on my side of the floor.

HARRIET. She has those expensive bunny rabbit slippers and she doesn't want to get the soles dirty. My god, Al, who could blame her? She'll come over now, if you keep your side neat. Why last night, after I'd cleaned the *mess* up and disinfected the floor, she walked across to the bathroom as calm as you please.

AL. What'd she make—number one or number two?

HARRIET. What?

AL. What'd she *make*—ca-ca or pee-pee?

HARRIET. Ca-ca, I think—What's the *difference*?

AL. Well you and her are such *buddies* now, I figured maybe ya went *in* there with her.

HARRIET. I did. She said she's afraid of toilets.

AL. Except she called it a *toidey.*

HARRIET. So . . . ?

AL. She's so goddamn *cute.*

HARRIET. Yes she is, Al.

AL. What'd she say about me that was so *fond*? She tell ya to buy me *food*, or what?

HARRIET. She just said you were fun and—

AL. *Fun*?!

HARRIET. —and that you weren't bad looking—

AL. Whudduya mean, "not bad lookin"? She said I'm not bad lookin or she said he's fun and he's good lookin? Which?

HARRIET. Not bad looking, she said, and wouldn't I like to move in and live on your side of the apartment like she lives on Ronald Nabors' side, and I said yes I would and she said that was good,

22

that that was good, that she was glad because she was very *fond* of you and she hoped you'd let me move in so I could keep your half clean like Ronald Nabors keeps their half clean so she could come over for a visit or walk to the bathroom by herself because sometimes when Ronald Nabors isn't here to carry her across your half she almost makes in her pants.

AL. Christ, that's real tough—

HARRIET. So if it's all the same to you, I'm moving in as of today.

AL. It's *not* all the same to me. Look what you've done to this place. I can't live like this. Where are my shoes?

HARRIET. In the closet. (*Al exits through the bathroom door and returns with a highly polished pair of shoes.*)

AL. What happened to my shoes?

HARRIET. I shined them.

AL. Okay, get out! (*Al goes for the duffel bag, strews its contents over the floor, and comes back to defiantly face Harriet.*) Whudduya thinka them apples?

HARRIET. Will you make love to me?

AL. . . . What?

HARRIET. Will you make love to me?

AL. (*Caught way off guard, stymied.*) You're eatin breakfast.

HARRIET. I'll finish later.

AL. The eggs'll be cold.

HARRIET. Cold eggs are my favorite. I love them when the butter's congealed. Will you? I think it'd be very good for both of us.

AL. *Are you outta your mind?*

HARRIET. *You don't have to yell . . .* (*Pause, she hears herself yelling.*) . . . she yelled. Why not? Because you're a fag, aren't you? Is that it? You're a fruit?

AL. Yeah, I'm a fruit.

HARRIET. No you're not. You're just afraid you won't be able to satisfy me.

AL. Oh sure.

HARRIET. Then why not? I have to know. I can take it. Why not, Al?

AL. Don't call me Al.

HARRIET. Well that's your *name*, isn't it?

AL. I don't like the way it sounds when you say it. "Al." Now get out!

HARRIET. How bout Big Al?

AL. (*Pause, take.*) Big Al?

HARRIET. Yeah—Big Al. Don't short guys always want to be called Big Somebody.

AL. I'm not *short!*

HARRIET. Okay okay . . . I don't know . . . all of a sudden I just felt like calling you Big Al, okay? It just seemed right or something. (*Trying it out.*) Big Al. Ma, I'd like you to meet my roommate, Big Al Simon. Big Al, this is—

AL. Will you please get the hell outta here! (*Al begins to choke himself as before.*)

HARRIET. *No!* And that won't work, that choking routine. I'm not budging until I know why you won't make love to me.

AL. (*Ceasing to choke himself.*) Then you'll go?

HARRIET. No.

AL. Come on!

HARRIET. *Uh-uh.* Because you want me to stay. (*Al comes for her, removes the tray from her lap. She stabs a last bite as the tray goes to the bed. Al grabs her by the wrists and yanks her to her feet. She breaks the hold and belts him in the stomach. He sags to the bed. She takes the tray and sits and eats.*)

HARRIET. I'm not going anywhere until I know why you won't make love to me.

AL. (*Breathing with difficulty.*) For one thing. I don't *love* ya.

HARRIET. I suppose you haven't ever made love to someone you didn't love before. Oh ho ho—You have and you know it! I checked your *record!*

AL. Yeah, okay okay—once, I admit it, I had this thing going with this girl Sharleen Hauser's Great *Dane.*

HARRIET. (*Stops eating.*) Stop it! Don't you know that hurts.

AL. You're beggin to be hurt.

HARRIET. What about that prostitute in Saigon? I suppose you loved her.

AL. I didn't go to bed with *her*—are you nuts? I just blew my nose on her head for a coupla laughs.

HARRIET. I think you're a virgin.

AL. Wanna bet?

HARRIET. Then why don't you get it over with and admit you think I'm ugly, ya coward jerk!

AL. Ya don't happen to appeal to me. Now how bout gettin—

HARRIET. No! (*Bending over him.*) Ugly! Say you think I'm ugly and I'm not good enough for a classy guy like you! (*She holds over him a moment, then exits hurriedly to the bathroom. He lies still a moment, then looks to Mandy, sleeping. After a hesitant moment, he goes to her. He looks back at the bathroom door, then presses his lips to Mandy's. She coughs. He presses his mouth to her pudenda through the quilt that covers her and Nabors. She stirs and he backs off.*)

MANDY. Oh—Al. I dreamed that someone had pressed his lips to my ga-ga.

AL. Mandy . . .

MANDY. Yes, Al, what is it?

AL. I gotta talk to ya.

MANDY. (*Same intonation as the first time.*) Yes, Al, what is it?

AL. I said, I gotta talk to you. Whudduya, got shit in your ears?

MANDY. Uh-uh. Cotton. (*She pulls a wad of cotton from one ear.*) I always keep cotton in my ears when I sleep so no dirt can get in while I'm in slumberland.

AL. Okay, look, I gotta talk to ya.

MANDY. Oh! Okay. Only I'll have to start brushing my hair while you do. We're going to a very big lecture this morning by . . . somebody. (*She starts brushing her hair and counting silently toward five thousand.*)

AL. Did you tell What's-her-name there—Harriet—that you're . . . what was it? —that you're very *fond* of me?

MANDY. Sure.

AL. Fond how?

MANDY. What do you mean?

AL. I mean, fond how?

MANDY. Well . . . *fond*, that's how.

AL. How fond?

MANDY. (*Pause.*) *Fond.*

AL. I don't know how to say this just right, Mandy . . . but I gotta have somebody I want. I can't take it anymore, not havin who I want.

MANDY. Oh, that's too bad, Al. Who do you want? (*Al buries his face in her pudenda again.*) Al, I'm trying to—Al, you're— I'm trying to—

AL. I gotta have you.

MANDY. Oww! Al, you're—

AL. Okay? (*Gets behind her, takes her by the sides of the face,*

25

silences her next line with a hand across her mouth.) Huh? Whudduya say?

MANDY. No! You can't just say—

AL. Don't say no! I said I *gotta* have ya. I didn't say can I—like . . . like there's some choice involved. I'm in trouble, Mandy, and you're the thing I gotta have. You gotta love me or I'm gonna kill myself.

MANDY. (*Pulling his hand from her mouth.*) You won't kill yourself Al. (*She puts his hand back to her mouth.*)

AL. Then I'll kill somebody *else.*

MANDY. Not *me* though, okay?

AL. I can't make any promises—unless you do. (*Al takes Mandy's face in his hands, kisses her forehead lightly, a cheek lightly, then her lips lightly.*)

MANDY. Eww! Al—your breath! (*Al holds her to him and she continues to stroke her hair and count silently all the while.*)

AL. (*Softly.*) Love me, Mandy. Okay? Come on—please.

MANDY. Al, I am betrothed more or less to Ronald Nabors.

AL. Break it off. You're very fond of me, remember?

MANDY. (*With a plastic smile.*) We're both very fond of you, Al. Aren't we, Ronny? (*She pokes Nabors who does not stir.*)

AL. Look at him! Whudduya *see* in him? I mean, you're beautiful, you're beautiful, Mandy, and you're . . . (*Pauses; there's really nothing else but this.*) . . . you're beautiful, and he's . . . I don't . . . I don't understand it! (*Pause. Mandy continues to stroke her hair and count silently.*) Ya know somethin, Mandy?

MANDY. (*Trying to think of something she knows.*) Uhm . . .

AL. I almost stayed in.

MANDY. Really, Al? Oh, that's interesting. In what?

AL. I almost re-enlisted. Ya know why?

MANDY. No, Al, why? Why did you almost . . . whatever you said?

AL. Re-enlist.

MANDY. (*Gayly.*) That's right.

AL. (*Taking her throat in his hands.*) How's this feel to ya, Mandy?

MANDY. To me? Not so hot. How's it feel to you, Al?

AL. Good. It feels good.

MANDY. You wanna know something else that feels *really* good, Al? Filling your mouth with chocolate pudding—the real gooshy

26

kind that Ronny makes—and then going squish squish like this. (*She demonstrates.*) It feels just like it does when Ronny drives his car into my garage.

AL. Lemme drive my car into your garage, Mandy.

MANDY. Oh no, Al. With Ronny's in there it would be too crowded.

AL. He drives a Volkswagen, for chrissake, and I drive a Buick. What kinda crowd could *he* make?

MANDY. (*Glancing at her watchless arm.*) Oh! —look what time it is. Ronny, wake up! (*Making a "time out" sign.*) I'm going to have to call time out, Al, so I can get my make-up on and get dressed. That was very interesting, Al. Let's make another conversation sometime when I don't have a very big lecture to go to. (*Al still holds her by the throat, though he has become detached. Looking up at him.*) There's time out on the field, Al. (*She presses his hands; they release. She gets up and goes to the mid-line.*) Eww! Who messed up? Al, did you mess?

AL. (*Absently.*) Yeah.

MANDY. Ronny, carry me across. (*Nabors does not stir.*) Al, Ronny's asleep. Could you put on his stuff and carry me across. (*Al turns on Mandy and shoves her violently into his half of the apartment. She cries out and begins to do a dance, as if she suddenly finds herself barefoot on a bed of red hot coals. She tries the bathroom door, finds it locked. Panicky.*) Come out of there, you! (*Harriet comes out. Mandy, doing her dance, is startled into a high leap.*) Oh!—Harriet—you scared me. (*Mandy barrels past Harriet into the bathroom, slamming the door. Harriet stares across at Al who stares detachedly at the door.*)

AL. (*Quietly.*) Okay.

HARRIET. Okay what?

AL. Let's . . . make "love."

HARRIET. (*Pause.*) Do you want to undress me or should I do it myself?

AL. No undressing. We get under the covers and I open my fly and you open yours.

HARRIET. That's quite romantic, isn't it?

AL. I don't wanna have to look at your body. I don't think it'd stand up to the competition. (*Pause. Then she gets under the covers. Al follows, covering them completely with the sheet and blanket.*)

HARRIET. Could you at least give me some semblance of fore play. I'm pretty big on fore play.

AL. Jesus, you're really put together.

HARRIET. Don't make fun of me here.

AL. No, I mean it. You got one of the all-time bodies.

HARRIET. Thank you.

AL. Is that enough? Can we get started now?

HARRIET. No.

AL. Now what?

HARRIET. I don't want it to be a joke. Make it nice. (*Mandy opens the bathroom door.*)

MANDY. Al—I'm done. Could you carry me back, please. I just washed my feet. (*Al goes to her, carries he back to her side, nuzzling his face in her hair.*) Ow—you're tickling. (*He puts her down.*) Smell my breath. (*Blows her breath in his face.*) You should give it a try—brushing your teeth. It makes your mouth feel all tingly.

AL. I'm gonna have sexual intercourse with Whozit now—Harriet —unless you don't want me to.

MANDY. Oh no—go ahead. You won't bother me. I'm just going to wake Ronny up so we can get to that big lecture on time and you and Harriet can intercourse your brains out. You really ought to brush your teeth first though. Your breath smells like a whole Indian village made doodey in there.

AL. I'll brush my teeth when I can have you.

MANDY. (*Patting his cheek absently.*) You're sweet, Al. (*She moves to awaken Nabors. Angrily, Al gets back under the covers.*)

AL. (*Loudly, for Mandy's benefit.*) Okay, where were we?

HARRIET. Uhm . . . you were here and here. I was here. (*Mandy pays not the slightest bit of attention.*)

MANDY. Wake up, Ronald Nabors, time to go to the big lecture. . . . Ronald Naabors! . . . (*Shakes him, shakes him, quietly and fearfully.*) Ronald Nabors? (*Pressing her hand over his heart a moment after burrowing under several books to find the spot.*) Oh my goodness! Al!—what does it mean when a person's heart isn't beating?

AL. Dead.

MANDY. What?

AL. He's *dead*.

MANDY. Oh . . . Then Ronald Nabors, my ex-roommate, is.

AL. Is what?

MANDY. Dead. (*Al and Harriet pop up. Harriet hurries to Nabors. She pushes some books aside and presses her ear to his chest. She rises and covers him with the blanket. She picks up the Froegle book.*)

HARRIET. He was reading Mr. Froegle's chapter entitled "The Odiousness of Obesity" last night. He was so upset that he searched these other books for a rebuttal. . . . He didn't find one, I guess.

AL. Serves him right.

HARRIET. How can you say that?

AL. Take those three words, arrange 'em, in a sentence, and spit 'em out.

MANDY. Oh Al, that's cute. (*Harriet returns to Al's bed, gets in, and covers herself to the neck.*)

AL. You're all alone, Mandy.

MANDY. I know it. Boy, it's a good thing you're here, Al. You better go brush your teeth now, and hurry.

AL. Ya mean it?

MANDY. Uh-huh. (*Al bustles off to the bathroom.*) I'm going to have to take Al, Harriet.

HARRIET. Yes, I know.

MANDY. I hope you won't mind.

HARRIET. Why would I mind?

MANDY. Oh—you're a swell sport, aren't you?

HARRIET. Oh yeah.

MANDY. You can stay if ya want. Would you like to stay? I'm going to have Ronny stuffed and put him back there in that empty spot and Al and I, we'll live over here and you could live over there because we'll need somebody to cook—Ronny always did that; and to clean—Ronny always did that too; and somebody to pay for all the groceries and stuff—Ronny always did that of course.

HARRIET. Of course.

MANDY. Of course . . . Of course what?

HARRIET. Of course I'll stay. (*Al enters with his hair wet and all slicked down, running his tongue across his teeth.*)

MANDY. Oh Al—how precious!

AL. Yeah?

MANDY. Oh yes! Harriet?

HARRIET. Precious.

AL. Can I do some touching?

HARRIET. Please do. (*Al gets on his knees and, starting at Mandy's ankles, begins to elaborately touch his way upward toward her belly under her nightgown, his eyes closed, moaning spasmodically with satisfaction as he goes.*)

AL. No more suicide for Al Simon!

MANDY. Al, Harriet's going to stay with us to cook and clean and pay for things.

AL. Uh-uh—*out*, Harriet! (*Harriet slowly rises from the bed, gets herself together, and starts for the door.*)

MANDY. Alsy, who's going to cook and clean and—

AL. You! Sshh!—

MANDY. Who!—

AL. —And I'm gonna quit school and get a good job.

MANDY. Doing what? What can you do? . . . Wait! (*Harriet is at the door when Al suddenly stops his trip up Mandy's body at her belly. She holds for several lines, then exits.*)

AL. What's this?

MANDY. (*Still caught up in who's going to clean, cook, etc.*) Wait, I said! What? Oh!—that. That's a cyst.

AL. The size of a baseball?

MANDY. Now, Al—

AL. A cyst! On *you*?

MANDY. (*Touching her belly.*) Uhm . . . yep—that's me.

AL. Can ya have it cut out?

MANDY. It's benign, Al, for godsake—what do you think!

AL. (*Rising to face her.*) Benign! Who cares if it's benign if it's the size of a baseball!

MANDY. If I have it cut *out*, Al, I'll have a *scar*. Now—

AL. But if you don't have it cut out, you'll have a cyst!

MANDY. (*Grimacing.*) Al, did you brush your teeth?

AL. Don't try to change the *subject*.

MANDY. Your breath still smells like a doodey factory! (*Mandy turns hatefully on Nabors.*) Thanks a lot, Ronald Nabors!

AL. You cheated, Mandy. (*Al takes Mandy from behind and begins to choke her again—this time, though, in earnest.*)

MANDY. Al, you're making my eyes bulge. I'll look like a frog. . . . Al . . . (*He finishes her off, lets her drop across Nabors. He stands. Momentarily Harriet enters. She surveys the scene. She lays Mandy out beside Nabors. She takes Al by the hand and leads him to his bed, puts him in it. She picks up a thing or two on the*

30

way to the kitchen. She puts the kettle on and opens the refrigerator, takes out two bottles of bouillon cubes. She holds them toward Al.)

HARRIET. Chicken or beef, Al? *(Blackout.)*

CURTAIN

PROPERTY LIST

2 beds, with pillows and blankets
2 easy chairs
Guns, rifles, knives, swords, bottles etc.
Dirty dishes, utensils, pots, pans etc.
Pipe (Nabors)
Felt pen (Nabors)
Books
Hair brush (Mandy)
Paper sack, with noose in it (Al)
Workman's gloves
Gas mask
Galoshes
Overcoat
Refrigerator, with moldy sandwich and beer in it
Slip of paper (Harriet)
Note pad (Nabors)
Pedicure set (Mandy)
Wastebasket
Overflowing paper bag
Empty duffel bag
Plastic bag
Clean pots, pans, dishes, glasses etc.
Breakfast tray, with flower in vase
Shiny shoes (Al)
Wad of cotton (Mandy)

DOING A GOOD ONE
FOR THE RED MAN

A RED FARCE
BY MARK MEDOFF

CHARACTERS

INDIAN
GRACE
LEONARD

DOING A GOOD ONE
FOR THE RED MAN

The desert just east of the Grand Canyon in Hollywood, Arizona.

An Indian sits cross-legged on an old packing crate before his rancid looking mud hut. He is dressed in worn and dirty Navajo clothing and holds a toy tom-tom. He stares fixedly before him. About him are various haphazard displays of pottery and turquoise beads and rings.

A young couple enters. They are Grace and Leonard. They are dressed in white with the exception of the camera on Grace's wrist, the hand mirror she bears before her, the lenses of her sunglasses, and the bag of golf clubs slung across Leonard's shoulder. Following their entrance, Leonard takes out his putter and begins to practice his stroke.

GRACE. (*Flowing in on a cloud of narcissism.*) It is an Indian, Leonard. I told you it was an Indian. Say something to it.

LEONARD. (*Following slowly and without interest.*) Hi-ho. (*No response from the Indian.*) Looks like a wooden job. Could be an ambush.

GRACE. Oh Leonard!

LEONARD. Yes, Grace?

GRACE. (*To the Indian.*) Hello, I'm Grace and this Leonard. We're on our honeymoon. (*No response.*) We saw you sitting here and we thought we'd stop and chat and perhaps learn something about our heritage and such.

LEONARD. We just saw the Grand Canyon. (*No response.*) It's a pretty big hole, isn't it? (*No response.*) Could you picture it as a cesspool?

GRACE. Leonard!

LEONARD. Yes, Grace?

GRACE. (*To the Indian.*) Then we left there and we were driving and we kept seeing Indians in colorful garb and I said they were

35

real and Leonard said they were hired extras in a travelogue about the picturesque Southwest.

INDIAN. *(Speaking simply, yet deliberately.)* Beads, pottery, rings.

GRACE. Oh Leonard, he spoke! *(To the Indian.)* I'm going to do a silly thing now. I hope you won't mind. I've always wanted to say "How!" to a real Indian. . . . How!

INDIAN. Take picture with me—cheap.

GRACE. Oh yes! Stand over there, Leonard. These can be our Christmas cards this year.

LEONARD. *(Moving without interest "over there", to Grace.)* What do you want me to do?

INDIAN. Got three choice: Can take picture of me tied to stake, you holding burning torch to pile of twigs—one quarter and one nickel.

GRACE. I'm not crazy about that one.

LEONARD. What else?

INDIAN. Picture of me circling your car on crummy old tricycle waving tomahawk—one quarter and one dime.

GRACE. Nooo, I don't think so. Leonard?

LEONARD. Ixnay.

INDIAN. Last one picture of me and you on horses—me in full Navajo chief outfit, you in cavalry colonel outfit; we smoking peace pipe and exchanging tokens of friendship. Cost one half buck.

GRACE. Oh yes—that's it!

LEONARD. *(Simultaneous with Grace's line.)* Great! We'll take that one.

INDIAN. Tough luck. Can no do. Horses die last winter.

GRACE. Oh, I'm sorry.

LEONARD. That's too bad. I really wanted that picture. *(Drifting off into fantasyland.)* It's funny, you know—but I always kind of pictured myself as a cavalry man . . . even if it was only a colonel.

GRACE. Could I just have a picture of you and Leonard shaking hands or something?

INDIAN. Cost one quarter.

GRACE. Go ahead, Leonard. Shake hands.

LEONARD. No—listen! *(Ramming his putter down the back of the Indian's shirt.)* He sits there and I do some flexing off his shoulder here. *(To the Indian.)* I been workin out like a maniac since two weeks ago. *(Leonard works into a tentative flex.)*

36

GRACE. Smile, boys. (*Neither Leonard nor the Indian smiles. Leonard searches for the right flex.*)

LEONARD. Specializing on my upper arms. You think it's easy, you're crazy.

GRACE. Ready?

LEONARD. (*Working finally into a tricep-bicep layout.*) I'd like to show you my workout chart so you could see what it takes to build upper arms.

GRACE. (*Snapping the picture.*) There.

INDIAN. That be one quarter. You pay now?

LEONARD. (*Retrieving the putter.*) Are you kidding? I keep a running tab wherever I go.

GRACE. (*To the Indian.*) You know something? Your face is a veritable map of America. It's just like Leonard's old wallet. (*Making the association.*) Do you have any leather goods?

INDIAN. Beads, pottery, rings. (*Grace begins to look over the goods.*)

LEONARD. How's business?

INDIAN. Not so good.

LEONARD. (*Moving in for a confab.*) Gee, that's tough. But then this is your slack season, I guess. I'll bet in the summer you really rake in the dough, huh? If you don't mind me asking, how much does a guy like you rake in during the year?

INDIAN. Hundred seventy-five dollar.

LEONARD. Holy cats! A hundred and seventy-five simoleans a week?

INDIAN. Year.

LEONARD. A year! Get out.

GRACE. Leonard, look at these darling beads.

LEONARD. Hold it—lemme get this straight here. You tryin to tell me you only make a hundred and seventy-five bills a year in the location you got, and with the merchandise you're pushin? Why you lyin redskin! (*Pause.*) Oh Jesus, I didn't mean that, it just slipped out. (*To Grace.*) I didn't mean that.

GRACE. Of course you didn't. (*To the Indian.*) I can assure you he didn't mean that. Why, Leonard was vice-president of Concerned Students on the Near Left last year.

LEONARD. Oh my God, why did I say that?

GRACE. We've been wearing African and Indian shirts to parties for almost a month now.

37

LEONARD. I feel sick.

INDIAN. Not matter.

LEONARD. Of course it matters.

INDIAN. Not matter.

GRACE. Let it matter!

INDIAN. Not.

GRACE. You mean you forgive him? (*The Indian nods simply, once.*) My God, he forgives you.

LEONARD. He forgives me.

GRACE. He's a saint! Leonard, he's a saint!

INDIAN. You buy authentic souvenirs?

LEONARD. Are you kidding? We'll buy plenty. (*To Grace, turning her loose to help him do penance.*) Buy!

GRACE. Leonard, look at these pots—

LEONARD. Buy!

GRACE. (*A miracle.*) They're clay! Look—Arizona Indian clay!

LEONARD. Oh my God! (*Then suddenly sober.*) Wait a second. All the sudden now I'm really concerned. My compassion for this suffering saint has exploded in the aftermath of my no-no. Okay, let's say you only make a hundred and seventy-five a year sellin this line. . . . What do you got goin in oil?

INDIAN. No oil.

LEONARD. Why you son of a . . . What do you mean, no oil?

GRACE. All Indians are in oil, aren't they? Isn't that part of the deal?

LEONARD. Sure it is. (*Squinting into the distance.*) What do you call that out there?

INDIAN. Desert.

LEONARD. Leonard means that derrick out there on the horizon. What do you call that derrick?

INDIAN. Cactus. Want cactus candy? Give to friends. They go upchuck.

GRACE. Oh yes, Leonard! Evelyn and Jay would get such a kick out of cactus candy.

LEONARD. Give us a crate.

GRACE. Not quite so fast, darling. (*To the Indian.*) May I sample a piece first, please.

INDIAN. No sample.

GRACE. (*Offended.*) Well!

LEONARD. No sample, no buy.

INDIAN. No buy. Make go upchuck.

GRACE. What is he saying?

LEONARD. What do you mean, make go upchuck?

INDIAN. Cactus candy. No buy. Make you puke. Plenty bad stuff.

LEONARD. (*A big condescending smile.*) Can I give you a little piece of advice? Now I just got my masters degree in Business Administration so I think we'll both agree that I know from whence I speak. You're never gonna get outta the hundred and seventy-five bracket goin about this selling thing like you are. Know what I mean?

INDIAN. Not know. (*Bored with Leonard's speech, Grace has returned to the goods.*)

GRACE. I'm picking some things out. Very nice.

LEONARD. I mean—look. Okay now, I'm you, right? Now I'm in business. I got a little roadside jobby here in Arizona, right? And I'm sellin . . . uh . . . beads and . . . rings . . . and pottery. All right now—

GRACE. And cactus candy. Don't forget that. I love these rings—

LEONARD. He said it makes you puke, Grace, didn't you hear him say about puking? I really don't foresee it as a biggie seller.

GRACE. (*Bringing Leonard in close for a private remark.*) He was merely being charitable because you wouldn't buy any. Pay attention, darling.

LEONARD. Okay. Whatever.

GRACE. And stand up straight. (*She helps him stand up straight. Leonard heads back to the Indian, Grace back to the goods.*)

LEONARD. So beads and rings and pottery and cactus candy. Now—

INDIAN. You want buy me?

LEONARD. What? —Wait a sec. Okay now . . . (*The Indian's line registers.*) What'd you say?

INDIAN. You want buy me?

GRACE. (*On whom the line registered immediately.*) Oh Leonard, let's!

LEONARD. What do you mean, buy you?

INDIAN. You buy me. Good deal.

GRACE. (*To Leonard.*) Pretty please.

LEONARD. Now lemme get this straight a minute. You're offering yourself to us for sale. Have I got that straight?

GRACE. (*To the horizon.*) Think of it—our very own human!

INDIAN. I live in your house, eat three square ones a day.

LEONARD. Listen, I don't think you know from whence you're giving me this crap. Don't you realize the deal you've got here?

INDIAN. Me starving.

LEONARD. Who you kidding?

INDIAN. Things really rotten.

LEONARD. What? You mean the competition is too keen?

INDIAN. Hungry all goddamn time.

GRACE. Here now—let's watch our language.

LEONARD. I don't see any other shops around. Looks to me like you control the territory.

GRACE. (*Grabbing Leonard and moving him away from the Indian.*) Maybe we could buy him and rent him to Frontierland.

LEONARD. Huh?

GRACE. We might even become an agency.

LEONARD. (*To himself.*) Leonard and Grace Rent-an-Indian.

GRACE. (*To the Indian, calculatingly.*) We were at Disneyland. I think we neglected to mention that.

LEONARD. (*Follows Grace's lead.*) Quite a bit of fun. Been there?

INDIAN. No been.

LEONARD. Damn cute actually.

GRACE. You'll be interested to know that they've got this authentic Indian show. With real Indians, you know, and they come out into the little friendship circle—right out of this darling little teepee, and they're just kids—teenagers—and they dance their crazy little heinies off to the wanton rhythm of the tom-tom.

LEONARD. Every hour on the hour. In between shows I'll bet they're in that teepee stowin away those hot fudgers, boy.

GRACE. It's quite nice.

LEONARD. The old chief, you know, he makes this speech about how the red brothers are happy that the white brothers have come to . . . uh—

GRACE. Integrate.

LEONARD. (*Competitively.*) —assimilate, as it were, the red man's traditions. Then he brings out the first dancer who does this thing about brotherly—

GRACE. (*Dropping out of the sell.*) Except, you know something, Leonard—they look so . . . bored or—

LEONARD. Bored!

40

GRACE. —or resentful.

LEONARD. Resentful! What are you—With the money they're rakin in and the assimilation that's goin on.

INDIAN. (*Simply.*) Atrocity.

LEONARD. What do they got to be resentful about? Are you— (*To the Indian.*) What'd you say?

INDIAN. Beads, pottery, rings, me.

LEONARD. What'd he say, Grace? Did he say—

GRACE. Atrocity. He said atrocity.

LEONARD. Atrocity. (*Angrily.*) Atrocity what?

GRACE. Not in that tone of voice, Leonard.

LEONARD. (*Moving in with a wagon load of righteous indignation.*) You know what's wrong with you? Your whole self-concept is screwed up. With your mercantile heritage and colorful traditions, you oughta be an ego-maniac, for chrissake.

INDIAN. Me die before go Disneyland.

LEONARD. They wear those fancy headdresses and everything!

GRACE. (*A shocking thought.*) Maybe it's all an act.

INDIAN. They hate.

LEONARD. Hate? Hate who? Who hates?

INDIAN. Indian hate.

GRACE. (*Jolted.*) Don't you see, Leonard—it's all an act. Why those dirty little fakers!

LEONARD. At Disneyland! Are you crazy? There's brotherhood oozin outta the woodwork. Those Indians love it. The ole choo-choo goes right by the ole teepee. (*Train whistle.*) Whooo-whooo! Oh sure, maybe they haven't got the kind of deal you got goin for you—oil and a chain of shops and all—but at least—

INDIAN. All Indian hate all white man. (*Begins beating tom-tom and chanting.*)

GRACE. (*Moving to Leonard.*) Leonard, perhaps we ought to get out of here. I thing you've done something.

LEONARD. Done what? Hey, lay off the drum routine, will ya? (*To Grace.*) I'm trying to help this schmoe and he's pounding his stupid drum and talking about hating. . . . Listen—Tonto! (*The Indian intensifies the beat at the mention of Tonto's name.*)

GRACE. Leonard, are you listening to me? I said let's get out of here before—

LEONARD. Okay, look—we'll buy you. (*Drumming and chanting stop.*)

INDIAN. You buy?

LEONARD. Yeah.

GRACE. Leonard . . .

INDIAN. Okay, you got new ball game.

GRACE. At least find out how much first, Leonard.

LEONARD. What's your price tag? And don't give me any west coast mark up.

INDIAN. Thirty dollar.

LEONARD. Thirty dollars! Christ, I can buy a slighly defective toy poodle for that.

GRACE. Maybe we should get a dog first. I'm really starting to wonder about this whole thing. Maybe just a souvenir or two—

INDIAN. I be son.

LEONARD. Son! You're old enough to be my grandfather. Just how old are you, Gramps? Don't tell me, Eighty . . . *six*.

INDIAN. Be thirty-one next Friday.

LEONARD. Bulldork! Don't gimme that crap—

GRACE. May I see you alone, Leonard. (*Reluctantly Leonard moves away with Grace.*) I honestly think a dog first, darling, and then we'll see about an Indian. Now, I'm choosing some trinkets and then we're—

INDIAN. I get car.

LEONARD. (*Swinging back to the Indian.*) Your own? Hell no. You'll borrow on the weekend.

GRACE. Leonard, what are you saying?

LEONARD. What *am* I saying? You're not going to be our son.

INDIAN. Be brother then.

GRACE. Well now, aren't we all brothers in the sense of men loving one another? (*Sings.*) Let freedom ring. . . .

LEONARD. Yeah, like that—that's fine. But not brother brother —like you just hang around the house and hit the refrigerator kind of thing.

INDIAN. What I be to you?

LEONARD. You'll be my . . . man.

GRACE. His valet.

LEONARD. Yeah. . . . My guy.

GRACE. Yes.

INDIAN. Kemosabe?

LEONARD. Yeah—kemosabe.

INDIAN. In other word, I be maid.

42

GRACE. Maid? No, silly. Ladies are maids. Men are—

INDIAN. Niggers.

GRACE. Well . . . yes. No! What are you talking about?

INDIAN. Maid nigger.

GRACE. No!

LEONARD. No! I mean a lot of them are . . . uh—

GRACE. Mexicans.

LEONARD. Sure. Mexicans, Puerto Ricans—

GRACE. What are we saying, Leonard?

LEONARD. What *are* we saying?

GRACE. Here: A lot of maids are white niggers—that's what we're trying to say.

LEONARD. Right. Plenty of maids are white niggers. What do you mean white niggers? Who started all this nigger stuff?

INDIAN. Indian and Nigger and Mexican get together.

LEONARD. (*Fearfully, but low key.*) What for? (*The Indian starts beating the tom-tom and chanting again. Leonard, to Grace.*) What's he pullin the drum routine again for?

GRACE. (*Heading for some goods.*) I'm making some definite souvenir commitments. We haven't given him any money yet. That could be the—

LEONARD. (*To the Indian.*) What do you mean the Indians and the Niggers and the Mexicans're gonna get together? *Could you lay off that, hey!* You've givin me some headache. (*The Indian stops drumming and chanting. Leonard, all business and quiet reason.*) Now what do you mean about this getting together?

INDIAN. What you think I mean?

LEONARD. I think you mean the three of you are gonna get together and . . . uhm . . . don't tell me . . . uhm . . . get the *Jews* cause they—

INDIAN. Not.

LEONARD. Not huh? . . . How bout . . . uhm . . . you're gonna get together and . . . uhm . . . get the *Catholics* cause they—

INDIAN. Not.

LEONARD. Not again. Uhm . . . I give up.

GRACE. (*Moving in.*) I don't give up. You're going to get together with the Negroes and the Mexican-Americans and you're going to build an army and you're going to wipe the white man off this continent.

43

LEONARD. (*Laughing.*) Don't be ridiculous. Jesus, Grace, you got some imagination—

GRACE. Aren't you?

INDIAN. First we torture his rotten white ass! (*Begins to drum and chant again.*)

LEONARD. First you're . . . Oh no you don't! Now listen, I'm tired of listening to this crap. Cut *that out!* (*Leonard grabs the tom-tom and destroys it maniacally. The Indian is stoic. Silence.*)

GRACE. Do you have a broom? I apologize for Leonard's childish behavior.

LEONARD. (*Pulling himself together.*) Okay, look I'm sorry, but I get so goddamn tired of hearing all this stuff about . . . Look, pal, I'm on your side. I'm—

INDIAN. You white son of a bitch. (*The Indian gets off his crate and disappears behind the hut.*)

LEONARD. Where's he going? (*Calling.*) Where you goin? (*There is no response from the Indian, so Leonard sets himself defensively at the corner of the hut, his putter raised like a club over his head.*)

GRACE. I'm not sure how that's going to work against an arrow, Leonard. (*The Indian returns from the opposite side with another tom-tom. Grace warns Leonard with a gesture and Leonard turns frantically and leaps at the Indian with an offensive yell which the Indian totally ignores.*)

INDIAN. (*Taking his seat again.*) You owe me for one General Custer tom-tom. This Warrior-of-Navajo-Nation model. How you like?

LEONARD. (*Takes up drum, looks it over, beats it a time or two.*) Nice. Gotta helluva tone. (*Leonard turns away and has a go at imitating some authentic, beating and chanting, stops abruptly, little embarrassed.*) I've always wanted to do that one for a real Indian—you know, just to get some authentic criticism. What'd you think? (*Returning the tom-tom.*) Never mind—you'll tell me later; maybe you can teach me a coupla solo numbers. Okay, now listen, getting back to this other thing—

GRACE. Pardon me, but do you have a toidey?

LEONARD. Grace, for chrissake, I'm trying to—

GRACE. I'm sorry, Leonard. (*To the Indian.*) Excuse me, but do you have a—

LEONARD. Uh . . . Grace, maybe you didn't—

GRACE. Leonard, I have to tinkle.

INDIAN. You need urinate? (*Leonard and Grace do a slow take.*)

GRACE. Why you disgusting savage! Did you hear what he said to me, Leonard?

LEONARD. You wanna watch your language, fella, or am I gonna have to take you downtown?

INDIAN. Take downtown, buy burger and order of fries.

LEONARD. Later. Now, I wanna clear up this miscon—

GRACE. Leonard!

LEONARD. Oh for chrissake! (*To the Indian.*) You got a toilet?

INDIAN. Have dumping grounds. Down in gully. Big hole. (*Points offstage.*) There.

LEONARD. (*To Grace.*) Go.

GRACE. (*Quietly offended.*) It's time to leave, Leonard. We'll take these few trinkets—

LEONARD. Are you outta your mind? You think I'm leavin with this kinda misunderstanding between us?

GRACE. I don't think you under—

LEONARD. *Use the hole, Grace!* I gotta straighten this son of a bitch out.

GRACE. I . . . am . . . not . . . going . . . to—

LEONARD. (*To the Indian.*) You wanna do me a favor? Just ignore her. Can we get together on that? (*Leonard ignores her. The Indian continues as before. After a moment, Grace exits haughtily to the hole.*) Now look, you gotta understand that just because I'm a white guy doesn't mean I'm not sympathetic to you people. Let's be—

INDIAN. Cram sympathy up ass.

LEONARD. No, now look, I'm not kidding about this. You can't make all white men guilty for the . . . uhm . . . you know . . . of a few.

INDIAN. Many.

LEONARD. Okay—many, few, what's the difference? The point is you can't just lump all of us together.

INDIAN. Indian lump.

LEONARD. Don't be ridiculous. See, that's just the point. Can I blame you for Custer's Last Stand? No, of course not. Well, in the same light, you—

INDIAN. You owe me two hundred million dollar.

LEONARD. For what?

INDIAN. New York.

LEONARD. Oh no you don't! Okay, so maybe twenty-four bills was a bid of a screwing, but a deal's a deal. See, that's part of what makes the democratic system run.

INDIAN. Screwing.

LEONARD. Deals!

INDIAN. How come no Indian ever President?

LEONARD. Oh, that's cute. I haven't been waiting for that one, right? Has a colored guy ever—

INDIAN. What about Jim Thorpe?

LEONARD. (*Fond memories of Burt Lancaster as Jim Thorpe.*) Hey—could that guy punt the pigskin!

INDIAN. You screw his brains out.

LEONARD. Are you kidding me? We made a movie about him and everything.

INDIAN. How many Indians star of tv?

LEONARD. (*Laughing.*) This is funny, you know that? You are just—Ahha! Tonto! What about ole Tonto?

INDIAN. Him Uncle Tom Indian. Disgrace to Indian nation.

LEONARD. (*Threatened, low key.*) What Indian nation?

INDIAN. (*Rhetorically, with the same intonation as Leonard.*) What Indian nation?

GRACE. (*Entering with enormous disdain.*) That's some hole. You want to hear about a hole, Leonard?

LEONARD. (*Fretting about the Indian nation business, distracted.*) No.

GRACE. That's a hole.

INDIAN. Big smelly hole.

GRACE. (*Moving in to remonstrate with the Indian.*) Smelly! Why that's . . . Just go down there, Leonard, and take a whiff of that hole. Do yourself a favor. (*To the Indian.*) That's disgraceful. Do you know that? Disgraceful. Can't you . . . can't you control yourself until you get home at night?

INDIAN. Home where?

GRACE. To your house or ranch or whatever you live on.

INDIAN. You funny lady. Ha ha. Me live here.

GRACE. You don't live here.

LEONARD. Of course you don't.

INDIAN. Hmm. That funny. All this time, think me live here. No wonder so unhappy: this not my home. If me not live here, where me live?

46

GRACE. That's what we're asking you. We're not saying you have to have us over or anything. We're just curious as to where you live.

INDIAN. Live here then.

GRACE. Now stop it!

INDIAN. Not live here, huh?

GRACE. No.

INDIAN. Hmm. (*Pointing.*) Live over there?

LEONARD. Listen. See: You tell us; we not tell you.

GRACE. (*Trying to speak his language, helpfully.*) We not know where you live; that be why we ask you where you live so you tell us and then we know too.

INDIAN. Live here. In this hut.

LEONARD. (*Coming in to the Indian's ear and speaking the first sentence very softly.*) You're about the dumbest bastard I ever met. . . . Now look! This isn't your house. This is your . . . office.

GRACE. Your stand.

LEONARD. Your store.

INDIAN. Ah—my store.

LEONARD. Right.

GRACE. Yes. Now . . . when you leave your store at night, where do you go?

INDIAN. Ah!

GRACE. He's got it.

INDIAN. Go to hole.

LEONARD. He hasn't got it.

GRACE. Let's try this: Where is your family? Squaw and papoopsies? Where them?

INDIAN. No family. Have Uncle Harry; him on road.

LEONARD. So that's how you rake it in, you crafty son of a gun, you. Pushing it on the road. Clever.

INDIAN. White man clever. Him screw ass off Indian. Pay Indian fifty cent for authentic mocassins, sell to niggers for eight bucks and to white man for buck-fifty. Him clever, boy. Really drag dumb ass Indian over proverbial coals. When we get you, we gonna bury one helluva lotta hatchets in your white head, boy. (*Here the Indian smiles, changing his expression for the first and only time in the play.*)

LEONARD. You're talking crazy, you crazy bastard.

GRACE. (*Suddenly going over to see the Indian's side.*) No. No,

47

Leonard, don't you see— (*During the next speech, Leonard is looking around for something to subdue the Indian with, motioning Grace to stay clear.*)

LEONARD. You're lying through your rotten teeth. Christ, why don't you see a dentist. Your personal habits stink. Look at your nails, ya slob. You look like a mechanic, for chrissake. You think settin the family up in a fleet of . . . what's—What're they drivin? Caddies?—You think settin 'em up in a fleet of Caddies and rollin in dough doesn't mean ya gotta take care of your teeth and nails? (*Leonard has found a lasso on the side of the hut. He tries a cowboy throw at the Indian but misses, so he steps behind the Indian, puts the loop around his shoulders and madly ties him up. The Indian puts up no resistance whatever.*)

GRACE. Leonard, what are you doing?

LEONARD. I'm tying this—

GRACE. Don't you see, Leonard?

LEONARD. Don't I see what?

GRACE. That we are merely lending ourselves to the perpetuation of the bitterness that this man feels toward the white man. My God, I suddenly see.

LEONARD. Oh, not your sensitivity routine, Grace.

GRACE. (*To the Indian.*) Do you understand? I'm no longer blind to your plight.

LEONARD. (*To the Indian.*) Don't get your hopes up. It's only a routine.

GRACE. Oh Leonard, how little you understand me, and how little I've understood our red brothers.

LEONARD. I don't know, Grace, you did this bit a lot better at our Chitlins and Collard Greens Festival last fall. (*To the Indian.*) All right now, for a coupla grand, we can turn this stand into a stunner. Got a minute? I'll just unfurl a coupla ideas here and we'll run 'em up the flagpole and see who salutes 'em. (*Leonard begins looking over the place, making notes on a small pad.*)

GRACE. (*Intimately, to the Indian.*) You've . . . you've opened my eyes. Do you understand? Oh, I know how silly this must sound, but I'm going to gain you a measure of retribution.

LEONARD. (*Calling from behind the hut.*) What are these walls—cement or cinder block?

INDIAN. Mud.

48

LEONARD. Mud . . . What kinda mud is what I mean? Cement or cinder block?

INDIAN. Mud.

LEONARD. (*Coming into view.*) If you're not gonna be serious, you can't expect the top results. What kinda beams you got? (*No response.*) Supports? You know, what holdee up roofee?

GRACE. That's Chinese, Leonard.

INDIAN. Grass and mud.

LEONARD. You got a real cute sense of humor.

INDIAN. And twigs.

LEONARD. Uh-huh. (*Wanders out of sight again.*)

GRACE. (*Intimately.*) He never has understood me now that I think of it. (*Pause.*) And now that I think of it, this is a hell of a time to be thinking of it. (*Pause, dreamily.*) You know how when you're young you think about the person you want to marry?

INDIAN. No.

GRACE. (*Oblivious of his answer.*) I was the same way—dreaming all the time. And, you know, I never wanted to marry a schmoe like Leonard. I always dreamed about marrying a poet or a professional golfer. That's why Leonard plays golf; I made him take it up. . . . God, he's lousy. (*Pause.*) Really a poet, though. That's really what I wanted. And we'd have a big old house in Vermont and every afternoon I'd take lemonade and fudge to his study, and he'd write sonnets to me and make me immortal. . . . What did you dream of? (*The Indian stares blankly at her, then resumes his position.*) Oh God, you're really touching me now.

LEONARD. (*Coming into view with a tom-tom.*) You ever thought of going the All-the-orange-juice-you-can-drink-for-a-dime route?

INDIAN. Never thought of.

LEONARD. (*Holding up the tom-tom.*) What do you get for this model?

INDIAN. Sitting Bull model. Plenty extras. Rawhide binding, fur-tipped drumstick—a steal at buck-sixty.

LEONARD. (*Laughing.*) A buck-sixty! You gotta be joshing. No wonder you're still in the Caddy bracket. Christ, with any kind of sound advice you'd have been driving Silver Clouds years ago. Now, if this were my business, I'd up this model to four-fifty. If she turned out to be the top of my tom-tom line, I'd tack on another buck and label her "Special Today Only." (*Puts tom-tom down beside the Indian, to Grace.*) You know what I could do with a place like this. Huh?

GRACE. Do it.

LEONARD. I could pull down maybe fifteen-twenty grand in this place with a coupla alterations.

GRACE. Do it, I said.

LEONARD. Do what? Buy him out, you mean, and we'll settle here?

GRACE. No. You buy him out and you settle here.

LEONARD. I don't get it.

GRACE. I'm leaving you, Leonard.

LEONARD. What about the wedding presents?

GRACE. Take them.

LEONARD. That's not fair. I want to be fair in this. I'll just take the waffle iron an what I think I can pass off as authentic Indian stuff.

GRACE. Untie him, Leonard. After nearly five hundred years, it's time he had his freedom.

LEONARD. Are you kidding? Not till I make a deal.

GRACE. (*To the Indian.*) My husband . . . my *ex*-husband would like to make a deal with you for your business. Let him have it. I can help you start a new life. I'll take you to Albuquerque. I have an uncle there who owns a cigar store. I know he'll give you a job.

LEONARD. Okay, what do you want for the building and your total inventory?

GRACE. (*To the Indian.*) Don't let him cheat you. And be sure to get his golf clubs in the deal.

LEONARD. I heard that! (*Guarding his golf clubs.*) One of the first things I'm putting in here is an authentic Indian miniature golf course.

GRACE. (*To the Indian.*) When we get to Albuquerque I'll give you our Volkswagen.

INDIAN. Me not touch German car with ten foot pole.

GRACE. Why not? It has a sunroof.

INDIAN. Father, three brothers killed in World War II.

GRACE. World War II . . . I'm afraid I'm not familiar with that one. Well, I'll give you everything in the U-Haul trailer.

LEONARD. Sounds fair to me.

GRACE. Untie him, Leonard, and let us be on our way. I'm sure you're as anxious to begin your new life as we are.

LEONARD. (*To the Indian.*) No funny business: my upper arms are like cast iron clubs. (*Unties the Indian, then to Grace.*) I want you to know, Grace, I appreciate what you did for me there.

GRACE. We've shared a lot, Leonard.

LEONARD. It was the least you could do.

GRACE. What will you do now, Leonard?

LEONARD. Not Leonard anymore—that's the first thing.

GRACE. Oh?

LEONARD. Uh-uh. Leaping Jolly Deer.

GRACE. Oh—very nice. Leaping Jolly Deer. What else? (*As Leonard goes on, Grace begins to look over the Indian, wondering how he might look cleaned up and "whitened."*)

LEONARD. Well, I figure between Williams and Flagstaff I'll throw up maybe ten billboards and hit 'em with the ole pooh-pooh the competitition routine. Tired-of-the-same-old-Indian-souvenirs . . . That one.

GRACE. I suspect that with all our Jewish brothers getting ready to send their children off to summer camp you'll do a fierce business in mocassins.

LEONARD. You think you're telling me something, Grace? . . . Now, on either side of the teepee, I put up in all caps: LEAPING JOLLY DEER'S—DIZ IS DE PLAZE. Huh?

GRACE. Oh yes.

LEONARD. Now—ready for this? You listening, Grace?

GRACE. Yes, Leonard.

LEONARD. Gas. (*No response from Grace who is looking at herself and the Indian in her hand mirror to see what kind of portrait they make.*) You're stunned, right?

GRACE. Automobile gas?

LEONARD. No, Grace, intestinal. Yeah, automobile! And hold onto your jock, Grace. I'm puttin in a car wash out back. (*No response from Grace who is doing a little work on the Indian's hair.*) Again stunned, huh? Get the picture, Grace: You're on the road to or from the Grand Canyon.

GRACE. And the car is filthy.

LEONARD. You got the picture. Bugs all over the windshield, maybe a bird in the radiator, a skunk squashed into your tire treads. And here you are coming from or going to one of the eight wonders of the world. You're feeling patriotic as hell, see? But here you are in this pig pen of a car. Suddenly—

GRACE. Suddenly . . . out there on that vast open desert . . . out there amidst the emptiness of this uncivilized land . . . it's LEAPING JOLLY DEER'S!

LEONARD. Yeah! FREE CAR WASH WITH FILL UP! The whole approach'll be to hit 'em in their Clean. If they're goin, they'll feel like they won't be despoiling the grandeur of the Grand Can. If they're leaving, the car wash'll act as a purging or somethin.

GRACE. Oh Leonard.

LEONARD. What do you think, Grace?

GRACE. It's brilliant.

LEONARD. Oh yeah, well it's not completely formulated yet, ya know.

GRACE. But what a beginning for you.

LEONARD. I mean I know I'm gonna have to put in a coupla crappers and level some of those damn hills and dales out there for parking but— (*Pause.*) I wish to hell I could divert some of the truck crowd out this way, but I'm afraid that's hopeless. Unless I put in one damn good takeout burrito stand or something. Well, what say we chow down some pimento cheeses and sign the papers. (*To the Indian.*) You got a mortgage on this place? Get the picnic stuff, Grace.

GRACE. Yes, Leonard. (*She exits.*)

LEONARD. (*To the Indian.*) All right, pal, let's go inside and get this spelled out on paper. I know you probably couldn't care less about contracts and all, but I like everything legal and above board. (*The Indian starts beating a tom-tom and chanting.*) Not now, man. You're gonna be big time, then grow up, will ya. (*The beating and chanting intensify. Leonard grabs the tom-tom and destroys it. The Indian takes up the other tom-tom and begins beating it. Leonard grabs this one and destroys it with careful fury. The Indian exits behind the hut.*) No more tom-toms! I'll look at all your goods in a minute. Oh hell.

GRACE. (*Entering with a picnic basket.*) I brought some jams too.

LEONARD. You know what I'm thinking might go in a place like this? Specialized items. You know, the kind of thing that's in big demand on a trip, but where do you get it? Like . . . uh . . . the rubber vomit, rubber dog turd line.

GRACE. Do you know what *I'm* thinking, Leonard?

LEONARD. Uh-uh.

GRACE. I'm thinking. Look at us, Grace Paul and Leonard Forsyth—doing a good one for the red man. (*They do a humble take on each other and enter the hut. We hear Leonard's voice, don't see them anymore.*)

LEONARD. Turn on the light, will ya. Oh Christ, he doesn't have any electricity here. That's carrying the authenticity thing too far, if ya ask me. (*The Indian comes into view slowly. He's carrying a beaten shotgun. The lights fade to darkness but for a low illumination on the door of the hut.*) Hey, ya crazy redskin, throw some light on the subject, will ya! (*The Indian pushes the door open and there is a blaze of shotgun fire into the hut, then sudden darkness.*)

CURTAIN

PROPERTY LIST

Packing crate
Toy tom-toms (3)
Assorted pottery, beads, rings etc.
Camera (Grace)
Hand mirror (Grace)
Bag of golf clubs (Leonard)
Lasso
Pad and pencil (Leonard)
Picnic basket
Shotgun

THE ULTIMATE GRAMMAR
OF LIFE

A PLAY IN ONE ACT
BY MARK MEDOFF

CHARACTERS

GOLDMAN
JAIME
WIFE

THE ULTIMATE GRAMMAR
OF LIFE

Geometric space. Oddly shaped risers of varying height, rising away from the audience, sliding into each other. On a riser C. *there is a skeleton bathtub,* D. R. *a double bed. A coat rack with a revolver and holster and a madras sports jacket hanging from it stands* L. *of the bathtub.* D. L. *there is a desk and chair.*

A telephone rings in the dark once, twice, a third time before the thirty year old Professor Goldman, standing D. C., *flaccid and balding, answers it by removing a cordless receiver from the pocket of his bathrobe, which he wears over slacks and a white unfashionable dress shirt. A light rises only on his face as he takes the receiver from his pocket, and simultaneously a light rises* U. R. *on the face of Jaime, a Mexican-American of approximately the same age, sleek and hard. He has a cordless telephone receiver to his mouth. Jaime is high up behind Goldman who does not look at him.*

GOLDMAN. Cogito, ergo sum.
JAIME. (*In heavily Mexican-accented English.*) Ju Goldman, man?
GOLDMAN. Well now, that just depends what Goldman you're speaking of. I am a Goldman, it's true, but whether I am—
JAIME. Ju Goldman, man—don bullsheet me.
GOLDMAN. I assure you I wouldn't bullshit you, sir. I'm not in the bullshit line. Goldman's the name, truth is my game—Remedial Grammar to be precise. Sounds like you could stand to take a class or two with me, sir. What's the deal?
JAIME. The deal ees I jus wanna tell ju dat I buy from jur Chaveron credit plate a set of tires an' a new battery for my '56 Chevrolet dat is in pretty crappy shape unteel I'ne fining jur wallet. (*Full light up on Goldman who slaps at a flaccid thirty year old buttock.*)
GOLDMAN. Hey, you stole my wallet, you spic! (*Catching him-*

self.) Oops! Forget I said that. I didn't mean that. Jesus, I just meant . . . I meant, You stole my wallet, you *bastard!*

JAIME. Not *steal!*

GOLDMAN. Okay okay, that's right, of course you didn't. You *borrowed* it.

JAIME. Found.

GOLDMAN. Horse dung!

JAIME. Oh jes, man, I fin' eet.

GOLDMAN. You chile-fingered *goniff.*

JAIME. Chingado, now I get hacked off! Ju no call *me* goniff an' geet away with eet, ju schmuck.

GOLDMAN. (*Whispering, feelings of soon-to-be-resolved misunderstanding welling up in him.*) Are you Jewish? Your excellent command of Yiddish leads me to make that deduction. Me too! I'm Jewish too. We're kinder. Brothers! You can't do this to a— (*But the phone is dead and the light blacks out on Jaime. Goldman, crying into the dead instrument.*) Christ! I mean I know you're out there and that you're getting people . . . But *me?* Surely you have lists! Surely you've got me down in the Amigo section. We're kinder, for chrissake! Hermanos! *Brothers!* (*Pause, staring into the dark, then soberly to himself.*) Maybe he doesn't know that. (*Crying into the dark.*) Hey! (*Goldman's beautiful and panty and bra-clad young wife is lit, u. L., staring guiltily at Goldman who never seems to quite "notice" her, try as she does to attract his attention.*)

WIFE. Hi. (*She waves childishly. Goldman screams, frightened, at the sound of her voice.*)

GOLDMAN. *Who are you?* (*Holds a pair of horn-rims to his eyes.*)

WIFE. (*Making her way down to him.*) Your wife.

GOLDMAN. Christ, you scared me—or maybe startled is a better word. Yes, you startled me—let's go with startled. (*Takes a professorial pipe from his bathrobe and pokes it in his face.*)

WIFE. I did it, I laid it down on a counter in a store where I was charging these undies and I went off without it . . . or something.

GOLDMAN. Eh?

WIFE. Your wallet.

GOLDMAN. My *wallet?*

WIFE. Uh-huh.

GOLDMAN. *What?*

WIFE. I lost your wallet . . . or something.

58

GOLDMAN. You *lost* my *wallet*?

WIFE. Or something. Uh-huh.

GOLDMAN. (*Shaking his head with calisthenic finality.*) Uh-uh.

WIFE. I *did*. (*She places her right hand over her pert left breast and tries to thrust a hunk of haunch into Goldman's peripheral vision.*)

GOLDMAN. (*His body launching a general twitch as he strains to control a fearful instinct to do irremediable physical damage to this woman.*) Oh well, what the hey . . . (*Bites into some bathrobe.*)

WIFE. You're not mad?

GOLDMAN. (*With bathrobe in his mouth.*) Mad? Why should I be *mad*? (*Spitting out the bathrobe.*) People make mistakes, right?—

WIFE. Uh-huh—

GOLDMAN. I mean, things get lost, *don't* they?—

WIFE. That's right—

GOLDMAN. Happens to everyone, isn't that *so*? (*Goldman's beautiful and semi-relieved young wife nods away, but just on a hunch that he is mad she strikes a pose and simpers:*)

WIFE. Lookey here. (*Goldman isn't in the mood for any of that, though, and instead of taking her in, he lunges at her, butting her in the solar plexus and sending her careening into the first level of risers; her head strikes the floor squarely and she's out for the count. Goldman, in his bathrobe, climbs into the bathtub, c., and displaces his anger to a battery-driven speedboat which he angrily races here and there in the tub, making appropriate angry racing sounds until his beautiful young wife comes to and approaches him cautiously, flashing at him portions of upper inside thigh. Goldman, though, is into his boat and some heavy thought.*)

GOLDMAN. It's a Mexican. A Mexican-American, I mean.

WIFE. A chicano.

GOLDMAN. You again. . . . That's right—a chicano. It's a chicano— (*And Goldman smashes a fist onto the top of his speedboat, blasting it into the bottom of the bathtub and killing it.*)

WIFE. (*Scared plenty, but trying to be helpful.*) We should call the police.

GOLDMAN. But we won't.

WIFE. No, we won't though.

GOLDMAN. Because I want to see what will happen.

59

WIFE. That's right. (*The phone rings. Goldman stands in the tub and pulls the receiver from his bathrobe. Light up on Jaime's face, D. L. this time. Goldman's beautiful young wife slips into the dark to change into something more comfortable.*)

GOLDMAN. (*Angrily.*) Cogito, ergo sum!

JAIME. How ju doin, man?

GOLDMAN. What's it to you?

JAIME. I'ne jus calling to tell ju dat I outfeet my seester in swaters por de upcoming weenter bout on jur J. C. Penney's charger machine plate.

GOLDMAN. (*With a legit tremor in his voice.*) It's not bad enough that we've taken it up the keister from the Aryans and Egyptians for six thousand years; now we really deserve it from you, don't we?

JAIME. Jes.

GOLDMAN. Incorrect answer. Ten off.

JAIME. To me, eet make no deef'rence between ju an' somebody else.

GOLDMAN. I'm an oppressed minority too, you insensitive wetback!

JAIME. Ju white, Jew boy.

GOLDMAN. I'm a card carrying liberal!

JAIME. Ju de enemy, madre, an' now I'ne carrying jur card. How ju like dem apples?

GOLDMAN. I'm practically a socialist, for chrissake!

JAIME. (*Chanting.*) Brown power—

GOLDMAN. I belong to the ACLU—

JAIME. —brown power—

GOLDMAN. —the NAACP—

JAIME. —brown power—

GOLDMAN. Get out of Vietnam!

JAIME. —brown power—

GOLDMAN. More government money for colored and tinted minority cultural events!

JAIME. Ju watch jur mouth, boy.

GOLDMAN. Don't you call *me* boy, you taco rolling son of a bitch!— (*But Jaime's light is gone, the phone dead. Goldman slams the receiver into his bathrobe and discovers his beautiful young wife standing there in a filmy negligee. He holds his horn-rims up to his eyes.*) Is that you?

60

WIFE. Uh-huh. I changed my apparel.

GOLDMAN. Do you see what you've gotten me into?

WIFE. All I'm wearing is this filmy negligee. Underneath there's naked.

GOLDMAN. (*Hissing.*) Sweaters! (*Goldman rakes his fingers through his thinning hair and comes away with a dozen or so dried up strands.*) Why do you think I'm losing my hair?

WIFE. Uhm . . .

GOLDMAN. Never mind, I'll tell you this time. But next time, be prepared. Because in six years you've lost—count them! —one engagement ring, two wedding bands, nine sets of pierced earrings, two household pets, and a rubber plant.

WIFE. And Volume Twelve from the Encyclopedia Britannica. Remember Volume Twelve?

GOLDMAN. Now he's buying *sweaters!*

WIFE. I wonder what size. (*Goldman's beautiful young wife climbs in to the bathtub and surrounds him. Goldman sinks to the floor of the tub and she plops her breasts on his head.*) If they're thirty-eights and there's a burgundy in the crowd, I've got dibzies. (*She rams a feisty breast into a Goldman ear.*) Guess what I'm doing to you.

GOLDMAN. *Driving me to the poor house on a tricycle!* (*Goldman slashes at his ear as if at a swarm of summer gnats. He leaps up.*) All right, I have to go to class now and put everything I've got into adjectival and adverbial restrictive clauses hewn out of the predicate's realm of reason *and I don't have a driver's license so I have to walk two miles to the university.*

WIFE. You don't have the piece of paper is all. But you do have license to drive. (*She gets around in front of Goldman and opens up her negligee.*) Look what's here.

GOLDMAN. (*Ignoring her.*) Taking no chances. Uh-uh. Cop force full of Mexes. No telling who's behind this—with my liberal rep.

WIFE. Did you say behind? (*Goldman's beautiful young wife spins around and tries to get him to peek at a rear exposure.*) Look. You're not looking. (*She sucks air through her teeth for all she's worth, blowing her bosom up to its very grandest. Goldman is off to the coat rack, though. He straps on the revolver and holster— very western—and slips into his ill-fitting twelve year old madras sports jacket. He tranfers the phone to the madras jacket and hangs up the robe.)*

GOLDMAN. I trust no one any more. From here on out I'm wary as a fox.

WIFE. I thought foxes were cunning.

GOLDMAN. Some are wary, some are cunning. *(Goldman's beautiful young wife exits the tub, slips his defense with catlike quickness, and presses herself to him, engulfing him in her open negligee.)*

WIFE. Don't take any chances, darling. What would I do without you?

GOLDMAN. *(Jolting himself free of her and checking to see that his revolver is loaded.)* You're right. I've got to think of others. *(Goldman's beautiful young wife leaps atop the bathtub, hitting a pose as she lands, quavering balance-wise for only a moment.)*

WIFE. Me. Think of me. Here, take some visual aid. *(Goldman, though, is wrapped up in getting into a somber longhorn head bolo tie he takes from a jacket pocket.)*

GOLDMAN. *(Detached.)* My challenge now is to figure out how I can kick that Mex's ass without doing damage to my liberal rep. Alright, I'm off. *(Goldman's beautiful young wife puckers up and Goldman absently shakes her hand. Light down on her and up on the desk D. L. Goldman crosses to the desk and sits, panting from the walk.)* Okay—here it is: What I'm going to do. I'm going to do no more than cancel all of my credit cards and offer him a little advice in exchange for my identification and the Captain Midnight secret decoder hidden in the secret compartment behind my American Express card. . . . And, of course, make him enroll in my Remedial Grammar Seminar for Semi-Literate Wetbacks. . . . And maybe give him just one shot in the kidneys. *(A phone rings. Goldman takes the receiver out of his madras jacket.)* Cogito, ergo—Christ, I can smell the green enchiladas on your voice from here. *(Light up on Jaime holding his receiver and standing in Goldman's bathtub.)*

JAIME. Listen, I don mean to, man, but I geet a teeket dis morning. I don got no driving's license, so I juse jurs. Ju got to be in court nine o'clock in de morning week from today or mail thirty-two bucks to court house eef ju admit jur guilt. Take it from me, ju was guilty.

GOLDMAN. (*A cracked smile flickering over his lips.*) A ticket?
Driving your own car?

JAIME. Das right.

GOLDMAN. (*Chortling delightedly.*) Pack it in, Pedro, you're
through.

JAIME. Das what ju tink, beeg nose. Eet don work. Ju know why
come?

GOLDMAN. (*His chortle catching like jagged toenail rippings in
his throat.*) Yes, because you got a ticket for driving without license
plates.

JAIME. Das right! An' with filed off serial number, ju dopey kike.

GOLDMAN. (*The real rub.*) And the cop believed *you* were me?

JAIME. He say, "When ju Hebes are going to learn ju can't rule
highway and byway like commie party?"

GOLDMAN. (*Biting off a pencil.*) Okay—that's the last straw:
I . . . I challenge you to . . . to a duel. *Name your weapon.*

JAIME. Jur wife. (*And the light blacks out on Jaime. Goldman
holds a dead instrument. Quicker than he could have said Jack
Robinson he's out of his "office" and into a high stepping, slow
motion lope, heading for "home," his street side thumb hooked into
the vision of passing motorists who continue to pass him. He
reaches his "home" after a trip or two across the stage and collapses
exhausted and dry heaving over the edge of the bathtub, in the
bottom of which he finds this note:*)

GOLDMAN. (*Reading the note.*) R9, K6, G4, A7, S9, R3, P7,
T2, G3, C1, H8, L5. (*Getting up.*) Where are you . . . (*Can't
remember his wife's name.*) . . . my wife? My wife! (*Goldman
charges around the "house," looking here and there. He stops* D. C.)
A suitcase full of her summer clothes are missing and my entire
stack of Xavier Cugat platters! (*Goldman grabs his groin, a sudden
pain arriving there.*) Aaugh! What's this sudden sense of painful
loneliness—or lonely painfulness—centering it's force in the vicinity
of my scrotum? (*Goldman cries out and crumbles to the floor,
clutching the note. In a flash, he holds the note before him.*) My
Captain Midnight Secret Decoder! (*Pause.*) Which I don't have.
(*Pause. Goldman looks around as if checking to see if anybody's
watching, then self-consciously he rises to his knees and clasps his
hands in prayer, having some difficulty remembering how the
fingers are supposed to mesh.*)

Dear God—or Lord, your preference . . . All right, so I'm a public agnostic; I think you and I both know that somewhere in me there's a very religious guy who's just been holding off until he had something important to ask for. Well, God, here I am on my knees beseeching you to help me decode this frigging message so I can save . . . (*Can't remember his wife's name.*) . . . my beautiful and innocent young wife from a fate surely tantamount to, if not worse than, death, Whachamacallit . . .: Amen.

(*No sooner has Goldman's "Amen" hit the airways than we hear a resonant, echoing and distinctly Southern "nigra" voice follow a clap of thunder.*)

VOICE. Well, hi, y'all kidderoos; y'all ready with your decoders for today's message? R9, K6, G4, A7, S9, R3, P7, T2, G3, C1, H8, L5. That's riiiight, baby! Decoded: "I got jur wife." Yes yes! (*Goldman leaps to his feet.*)

GOLDMAN. (*Shrieking at the heavens.*) *You stupid moron! I know he got my wife. I needed you to tell me that?* (*Goldman whimpers and gets into the bathtub. Pause, picks up and discards his boat, folds his arms resolutely.*) I'll just sit here and I'll wait, because I know that if I wait the guy'll call. That's what I'll do. (*Not so sure that's what he should do. The lights dim. Goldman waits. He scratches his chest absently. The lights dim some more. Goldman starts to doze off. He awakens with the pain in his groin and grabs himself, crying out. The phone in his jacket rings. Guiltily he throws his hands away from his groin.*) Yeah—cogito, ergo sum! (*In the background behind Jaime's lighted face, U. R., we hear the sounds of Goldman's beautiful young wife moaning quietly and a ukelele combo belting out some Hawaiian rhythms.*)

VOICE. (*Female.*) I have a long distance call for Goldman, pleeuz.

GOLDMAN. Just Goldman—or Professor Goldman?

VOICE. Just Goldman. I'm sorree, I know how these things can be. Is this him?

GOLDMAN. He.

VOICE. So sorree. Is this he?

GOLDMAN. (*Angrily.*) Yeah, okay—this is he.

VOICE. Go ahead, pleeuz, and I do hope you enjoy your call.

GOLDMAN. *Where's my wife? What have you done to her?*

JAMIE. Das por me to know an' ju to fin' out.

GOLDMAN. *If there's any carnal knowledge involved here—*

(*Goldman reins himself in, works up a warm-as-toast little drawl:*) Where are y'all?

JAIME. Oh no ju don, hose nose. I'ne not making eet so easy. I'ne telling ju only dis: De whole thing, eet is on jur TWA charger machine card, an' I won to say gracias mi amigo from de both of us. (*Light down on Jaime.*)

GOLDMAN. Operator! Operat—

VOICE. Yessir? Did you enjoy your call?

GOLDMAN. Trace that call!

VOICE. I'm so sorree, sir, but I cannot do that unless you are a member of one of our law enforcement agencies or a person of particular importance in his own right.

GOLDMAN. I'm a professor of Remedial Grammar at our very own university.

VOICE. Oh!—well in that case, Pro-fessor, your call came from room 1208 of the Honolulu Hilton. And aloha to you from all of us on the twelve to eight shift.

GOLDMAN. Now it's *Hawaii!* Okay, I'm through being Mr. Nice Guy! (*Blackout. Lights up on Jaime and Goldman's beautiful young wife in the bed, D. R. copulating under a tent of sheet and bedspread with appropriate moanings, backed up by the sounds of the uke combo, their gyrations and moanings on the beat of the music. Goldman bursts onto the scene, revolver in hand. Recognizing their posture instantly, sticking the gun up against Jaime's rising and falling ass, the gun rising and falling, the music stops on the line.*) Stop raping my wife!

JAIME. (*Peeking out of the tent at Goldman.*) Rapes? Who rapes?

WIFE. (*Pounding on Jaime, covered by him and the tent.*) Don't stop! Don't stop!

GOLDMAN. (*Leaning down to the tent, calling to her.*) What do you mean, Don't stop?

JAIME. (*To Goldman.*) Por favor, ju excuse un momentito, I finish up pronto, jes?

GOLDMAN. No! Now you cut that out.

WIFE. No no no! Fill me up! Fill me up!

JAIME. Please—ju mus' seet down un momentito; I have my duty. Please to finish some crab salad we dint got time por to eat. Ju mus' be hongry.

GOLDMAN. They fed us on the plane.

JAIME. Please to help jurself to some very nice Gallo Piñada. Now, excuse me, I got to go here. *(Jaime dives back into the tent. Goldman picks up a glass of wine off a serving cart R. of the bed and wanders around until they wrap it up with simultaneous cries and a down shifting of moans. Jaime, popping his head out of the tent.)* Please to hand me jur bathrobe.

GOLDMAN. *(Snatching the robe off the end of the bed.)* My bathrobe!

JAIME. Ju excuse me again, please, but I don' got some bathrobe, so I fin' jurs.

GOLDMAN. *(Throwing the bathrobe at Jaime.)* Okay, but that's the last time I'm excusing you. Now, say your prayers, you prick —pardon the alliteration and no pun intended. *(Jaime slips into the bathrobe and falls to his knees, clasping his hands before his chest. Goldman is caught up by Jaime's hand-clasping technique.)* Are you planning on praying?

JAIME. Jes.

GOLDMAN. I thought you were supposed to mesh your fingers together like this.

JAIME. Das de old way. I fin' personally that I get better results eef I clasp dem like dees.

GOLDMAN. *(Pause, then remembering his business.)* All right, get on with it.

JAIME. Dios mio, please to let this woman bear my children. I love her as my life.

WIFE. *(Rising to her knees, the tent around her, enfolding Jaime to her.)* Oh Jaime, yes yes. Oh yes, Jaime, yes. *(Goldman's gun droops. Clinging lasciviously to Jaime's back, her nose nuzzling in his sleek and obscenely abundant black hair.)* I'm staying with Jaime. We're finding a thatched hut on the beach here and we're opening a taco stand and the amount of naked oceanfront cavorting will be staggering.

GOLDMAN. *(To an absent fourth.)* I'm losing my hair. Who'll have me?

JAIME. Eef I could, I would give to ju my entire hair in trade por dees woman.

WIFE. *(Popping her head out of the tent where she had disappeared to slip into a bikini.)* Eewww, who would want you? Nobody wants a baldy. *(She disappears to finish dressing and Goldman moves to the tent to launch his major attack. He takes his*

66

beautiful young wife by the shoulders through the covers, and says:)

GOLDMAN. This man isn't Jewish.

WIFE. Neither am I.

GOLDMAN. Huh?

JAIME. She no Jew, an' get jur kikey hands off from her shoulders. *(Belted square in the kisser by this reminder, Goldman removes his hands and reels away.)*

GOLDMAN. My God, that's right. And my grandparents sliced me out of their will when I married you. *(Goldman takes the covers fearfully from her head:)* I remember you now. Jesus, I'm out a couple of grand and I'm seriously asking myself was it worth it. *(Moving away.)* I mean, is this what my ancestors suffered the Pharoahs for? Is this the kicker for the Inquisition, not to mention but in passing World War II? Holy mackerel, this is some payoff for my left wing leaning, for the perilous position I've placed myself in by unstintingly backing underdogs the world over.

JAIME. Who ju keeding, man? Ju hate us jus like we hate ju— *(And Jaime knees Goldman for all he's worth square in the nuts.)* An' das por all jur lousy pawn stores in Jew York.

WIFE. *(Hovering over Goldman in her bikini.)* I never wanted to marry you in the first place. It was my mother. As soon as she heard Jewish and doctor, she shoved me into it. What'd she know between medicine and remedial grammar? All she was thinking about was her gall bladder. To her all doctors did gall bladders. All I ever wanted was to marry a plumber or a mechanic—someone who could do something with hands. *(Goldman navigates the trip to his knees and reaches out to his beautiful young wife with the hand that isn't squeezing his testicles.)*

GOLDMAN. *(Rasping beseechingly.)* I fondle. I'm a good fondler. Remember?

WIFE. Who's talking about a coupla cheap feels on a third date?

JAIME. *(Blasting Goldman in his kidney, sending him reeling.)* An' here is por internacional banking cartel!

WIFE. *(Grabbing Goldman by his bolo tie and screaming in his anguished face.)* I want plumbing and automotive and rough—not an occasional fondle and predicate adjectives!

JAIME. *(Driving fists into Goldman's ribs, causing great pain and shortness of breath for Goldman.)* Here is por cornering de market on doctor, lawyer, an' Indian chief.

GOLDMAN. (*Gasping.*) I never wanted to be a doctor. (*To Jaime.*) Just like you never wanted to be a . . . what?

WIFE. (*Cooing, pressing Jaime's hands to her pelvis.*) Grease monkey. Oh, handsies. *Handsies!*

GOLDMAN. Okay, like you never wanted to be a grease monkey, I never wanted to be a doctor.

JAIME. What ju wanted to be—presidente de commie China?

GOLDMAN. A Greyhound bus driver.

WIFE. *What?* You never told *me* that.

GOLDMAN. (*Getting to his feet, taking Jaime aside, their backs to Goldman's beautiful young wife.*) Listen to me, don't you see? We can't go on getting each *other.* That's just what the bastards want. We've got to unite.

JAIME. Weeth ju as el presidente—uh-uh, forget eet.

GOLDMAN. No—what do I care? I'll be treasurer for all I care.

WIFE. What's this about *bus* driving?

JAIME. Eet's no good. Ju responsible for plight of brown man in U. S. of A.

GOLDMAN. I'm not either, you stupid asshole!

JAIME. Oh jes.

WIFE. Single or double deckers?

JAIME. I'ne telling ju what though. Ju get dem an' we get ju an' den everybody be happy, jes?

GOLDMAN. No!

JAIME. (*Clutching Goldman's beautiful young wife.*) An' I start by taking jur wife.

WIFE. (*Kneading her perfect buttocks with Jaime's grease-mapped hands, over Jaime's head at Goldman.*) Cross country or short runs?

JAIME. If ju such a good guy, ju be glad to help me out.

GOLDMAN. What about *me* though? How about you being a good guy and helping *me* out?

JAIME. I never play like to give crap por ju. I got too much problems to worry about ju.

GOLDMAN. What about the Golden Rule?

JAIME. All screw me, I screw back whenever I get de chance. Golden Rule.

GOLDMAN. What about the Ten Commandments, perdition, mortal sin—

JAIME. I not fall for dat crap no more. No mas, madre. I geet

68

when I can. I worry about Him when I geet dere. Somebody got to fix His car, jes?

GOLDMAN. (*To himself.*) Why bother? What's this doing to what's left of my hair?

JAIME. Ju should try a good protein shampoo.

GOLDMAN. You think so?

JAIME. (*Looking into Goldman's hair.*) No, I take eet back. Ju got no hope. She's rotting to the roots. Das tough.

GOLDMAN. Well, I guess that wraps her up. (*To his beautiful young wife, as he tears the heads off of several well kept fingernails, spits the pieces out, wipes his palms across the floor, and then sticks the messy things in her face.*) I just want you to know that I'll be back. As of tomorrow, I'm into a heavy weightlifting program and I'll be in the Greyhound program within the month.

JAIME. Don' forgeet to pay dat ticket I get or ju going to be in beeg trouble.

GOLDMAN. That's right—thanks.

WIFE. (*Whispering seductively, then tunneling her tongue into Goldman's ear.*) Could you make it moving vans instead of buses?

GOLDMAN. (*Responding in a way he'd forgotten to the tongue in his ear.*) Moving vans it is!

JAIME. (*Shoving Goldman's beautiful young wife away from Goldman and advancing on him.*) Ju get close to my woman an' I cut jur heart out.

GOLDMAN. (*Retreating.*) You scare me now, but let me come up with the biceps to wheel a semi and trailer around a cloverleaf and there'll be a new tension between us. (*Quicker than a flash, Jaime is out with his blade. Goldman stands his ground, tries out a little shoulder flex and spit-suck through his side teeth that feel like gangbusters.*) I'm going to be coming back for both of you, if you get my meaning.

WIFE. (*Whispering privately to Goldman, getting between him and Jaime.*) Call me when you've got your own rig. (*Furtively she slips Goldman's wallet into his front pocket and in so doing touches his member, stirring in Goldman another feeling he'd forgotten he ever experienced. He feels faint and goes to one knee, burying his face between his beautiful young wife's thighs. Whispering still.*) Jockey shorts. And preshrink them, then dry them in the oven at 450 for two hours.

JAIME. No helping! (*Jaime takes Goldman's beautiful young wife by her lustrous hair and whips her to the bed where she sprawls, emitting a sharp sound for service. Flicking his blade at Goldman.)* Ju—out! Somebody, she's calling me. *(Goldman backs D. L.)*

WIFE. *(Calling after him as she pops under the covers and begins to undress.)* Drop the *g*'s from all your *ing* words and cultivate the use of *ain't* and *none*.

GOLDMAN. I ain't stupid. I'm doin it as a now. *(Testing it.)* Doin. Doin.

WIFE. Sandpaper your hands! *(Goldman moves D. L. of the desk and the lights fade from the "hotel room." Goldman comes to the corner of the stage and stands a moment, then slowly, as if poking fruit to test it's resilience, he pokes at his groin and finally presses his hands firmly there.)*

GOLDMAN. Whudduya know . . . the ultimate grammar of life. And I got it. *(He holds a moment, then, as if he's driving and shifting a semi, he clutches and winds out his engine as he exits U. into the darkness. Blackout.)*

CURTAIN

PROPERTY LIST

Skeleton bath tub, with battery-driven toy speedboat
Double bed, with bed spread
Coat rack, with revolver in holster and madras jacket
Bolo tie, in pocket of madras jacket
Desk and chair
Telephone receiver, in bathrobe pocket (Goldman)
Telephone receiver (Jaime)
Switch-blade knife (Jaime)
Horn-rimmed glasses (Goldman)
Pipe (Goldman)
Pencil (Goldman)
Serving cart, with glass of wine on it
Wallet (Wife)
Note, in bath tub

THE WAR ON TATEM

A PLAY TOLD FOR SPEECH, MIME, AND DANCE

BY MARK MEDOFF

In memoriam:
The Tatem Perch, 1951
Bud, Big B.R., Cissy, Jay, Frank, Gary

CHARACTERS

LOUIE DUNBAR

HERMAN

EDDIE BERKOWITZ

BOYSY DUNBAR

SISSY FRANKEL

RICHARD RICHARD

MURRAY MOSKOWITZ

MYRON

THE WAR ON TATEM

The Tatem Perch, a very untough looking gang of five boys and one girl, are stacked in geometric configuration through the platform levels of an otherwise bare stage. The ages of the actors playing the children should be fairly consistent and at least in the late teens, early twenties areas since Louis Dunbar, the narrator and the character who is performing this public exorcism of a long lingering demon, is approximately twenty when the play ends. It would not be at all disturbing if the actors were elderly. Louis Dunbar moves among the Perch, using them now and whenever he can to aid visualization of his narration. The style of the play should be strongly oriented to mime and dance, conveying as nearly as possible the fluidity of a dream.

LOUIE. War came to Miami Beach, to Tatem Waterway Drive, on an August morning when I was ten, and no one was more surprised than I was—me who had been preparing diligently for it since June when I formed the Tatum Perch to protect myself and my brother Boysy and some others on our block from local marauding gangs—of which there were none. (*Pause.*) Until this particular morning, that is, when incredibly there was a kid named Myron with a gang named the Tatem Waterway Louse Drowners. (*The Perch respond now as Louis Dunbar tells it, miming, "dancing" variegated but synchronized anxieties in the face of the foxhole-digging, fist-shaking Louse Drowners.*) They appeared in the empty lot down the block next to the Tatem Waterway Apartments' Swimming Pool and Cabana Club, and they were digging foxholes and shaking fists in the direction of the duplex we shared with the Moskowitzes, beside which sat a Hopalong Cassidy pup tent, into which the Perch were crammed. (*The Perch move D. C. in a concentric circle, their movements stylized and balletic, and create of themselves a crammed pup tent.*) I didn't like what I saw through the flaps of that pup tent and I didn't like it even more when the messenger showed up on his bike to announce that it was war to see who ruled Tatem. *(Through the audience and up a ramp comes Herman, riding a pantomimed bike. He slams on the brakes, skids in close to Louie Dunbar—who is on his knees in the mouth of the tent—and does a flying dismount. The rest of the Perch are stacked behind and around Louis Dunbar.)*

HERMAN. Louis Dunbar?

LOUIE. Yeah?

HERMAN. It's war, Louie Dunbar, to see who rules Tatem.

LOUIE. *(Coming slowly from the tent, followed by the other Perch and followed especially by Eddie Berkowitz who tends to shadow Louie Dunbar like some unattached and useless appendage.)* What? . . . War? . . . Oh well . . . uh—no, I don't think we're in the mood for one if it's all the same to you. And then the messenger laughed like my brother Boysy laughed when he was trying to drive me crazy—loudly and shrilly, like someone who wasn't at all in the mood for working up a loud, shrill laugh. Like this: *(Boysy laughs loudly and shrilly. Herman unkindly imitates Boysy's loud and shrill laugh.)*

HERMAN. *(Solemnly.)* King Myron has spoken.

LOUIE. King?

HERMAN. King *Myron,* kid. I'm Prince Herman.

LOUIE. Prince Herman. Hey, that's good, no kiddin. The way we're set up over here is that I'm Commander-in—

HERMAN. When ya wanna fight? *(Herman dance-boxes around Louis Dunbar, throwing a few combinations. No physical contact is made.)*

LOUIE. What? . . . Well, I mean actually we don't wanna fight anytime. What it is, see, is we're set up as mainly a defensive force—

HERMAN. *When?*

LOUIE. Looooook, why fight? Right, gang? *(The Perch are quick to agree.)* We could all be friends. *(Louie Dunbar drapes a friendly arm across Herman's shoulder, but Herman leaps away, getting his bicycle between himself and Louis Dunbar.)*

HERMAN. Uh-uh! King Myron's from Brooklyn . . . *(An undercurrent of several "Brooklyns!" from the Perch.)* . . . and he knows better'n to have two gangs occupying one block. It's too *crowded,* if ya get my *meaning,* Louie Dunbar. *(Herman jams a finger vengefully up his nose—to which Sissy Frankel makes a disdainful*

76

retching response.) You got till two o'clock to make a time. (*Herman rips his finger out of his nose into a damp, lethal looking pointerstick and takes off in a good run, flips onto his bike, and peddles with grim intent back over the ramp and through the audience, crouched over in a way that makes Louis Dunbar hate his guts. Richard Richard, the youngest of the Perch and oblivious to the exigencies of war, waves goodbye. Boysy punches Richard Richard in the stomach and rabbit punches him to the ground.*)

LOUIE. This is Miami Beach! Not Brooklyn, ya moron! Who cares about . . . Listen! Hey, I . . . POOP! (*Louie Dunbar turns to the Perch who turn to him. They freeze, all but Boysy and Richard Richard mature enough to know enough to be reasonably scared to death. Louie Dunbar breaks.*) If it were during the school year, I figured I could avoid the whole thing on account of studying and Hebrew School and it just generally being a very impractical time for me to get my skull bashed in. But it was summer, and to make things worse somehow, Richard Richard's father had just got back from the Korean War with a lot of swords and junk that we spent a lot of time sneaking into the Richard house to look at. In short, I didn't see any way I could just forget it unless I could suddenly need an operation or get hit by a bus or something. And then there was Boysy: he was only eight and I was ten and Commander-in-Chief. (*Louie turns his head back to the frozen Perch a moment, then looks off.*) I'm trapped. So I decided my only hope was to call for a vote of confidence and lose—something I wouldn't stand for for five minutes. But I called for a vote of confidence anyway to combat Murray Moskowitz' latest challenge to the Commandership: Murray Moskowitz had brought a double-pack bag of barbeque chips that morning and Sissy Frankel said because he shared he should be Commander.

MURRAY. I got barbeque chips here and everybody gets eight of 'em.

LOUIE. Okay, we're havin a vote of confidence. Everybody in the tent. (*The Perch make a pup tent of themselves. Louis Dunbar crams himself in last, forcing his way between Sissy Frankel and Murray Moskowitz.*)

SISSY. (*Cranky at being separated from Murray Moskowitz.*) Ouch! Watch out—Louie Dunbar, I'm—I was *sitting* there, Louie Dunbar.

LOUIE. Okay. What wants me for Commander-in-Chief raise their hand. (*Only Eddie Berkowitz and Richard Richard raise their hands. Sissy Frankel is suddenly occupied with the injury Louie Dunbar inflicted on her when he crawled between her and Murray Moskowitz. Boysy is trying to pass out by holding his breath, and Murray Moskowitz is looking out of the tent, raptly attentive to something far out in the sky.*) Who else? Raise their hand. (*Eddie Berkowitz thrusts his hand in front of Louie Dunbar, anxious that Louie Dunbar be fully aware of his loyalty.*) Yeah yeah, I got you, Eddie. Thanks. But who else. . . . Raise their hand. (*Nobody else raises his hand. So, as if he considers the possibility extremely remote, Louie Dunbar asks:*) Who wants Moskowitz? (*Murray Moskowitz and Sissy Frankel raise their hands. Sissy rams hers into the air, but Murray Moskowitz only raises his a little bit, bringing into play a brand of modesty that drives Louie Dunbar to belch in Murray Moskowitz' ear.*)

SISSY. Eew! Louie Dunbar, that's disgusting!

LOUIE. (*Turning on Sissy Frankel.*) Look who's talking.

MURRAY. (*Quietly, to Boysy.*) Here, Boysy, why don't you knock off the resta these chips for me, pal. (*Louie Dunbar turns on Boysy who dives into the last of the chips. Louie works up a yawn and says:*)

LOUIE. Who ya want, Boysy, me or Moskowitz, for Commander? (*Out of the corner of his eye, Louie Dunbar glimpses Murray Moskowitz surreptitiously pointing to himself and mouthing, "I gave you those chips." Boysy sticks a finger to his mouth and says "Uuuuuuuuuuuuubbbbbmmmmmm" for several long seconds. Murray Moskowitz continues to point at himself as he leans out the opening of the tent in an attempt to convince Louie Dunbar he's listening for something. Suddenly Louie Dunbar turns on him.*) Whacha doin, Moskowitz?

MURRAY. Eh?

LOUIE. I said, wha-cha do-in?

MURRAY. Oh. I thought I heard my mother callin me for lunch.

LOUIE. Havin that brown goulash today, Moskowitz?

MURRAY. How'd ya know?

LOUIE. Cuz you're the only guy in the Perch that his mother never has everybody over for lunch cuz she always says all's you're havin is that brown goulash.

SISSY. Are you saying something against the good name of Murray Moskowitz' mother, Louie Dunbar?

LOUIE. I'm saying she sure must make a lotta brown goulash, boy. (*Boysy sucks in a good breath and lets go another "Uuuuuuuhhhmmmm."*)

MURRAY. (*Patronizingly, to Boysy.*) You're gonna run outta breath, Boysy, and we wouldn't want that to happen, would we, gang? Uh-uh. How bout quit saying "uhm" and castin your vote for the new Commander. (*Boysy let's go another "Uuuuuhhhhmmmm."*) That's really good, Boysy. Doncha wish ya could do that, gang?

RICHARD RICHARD. I don't.

MURRAY. Who's it gonna be, Boysy, for the new Commander?

BOYSY. (*Sucking in a huge breath and exhaling the line.*) Louie Jerkface Dunbar.

LOUIE. (*Quickly.*) I'm Commander-in-Chief. (*At first Louie Dunbar is greatly relieved to have his burdens reaffirmed, but now more burdened by the prospect of war his relief dissipates.*) Great. (*Murray Moskowitz crawls out of the tent, disappointed.*) Where ya goin?

MURRAY. I gotta walk this off a minute.

SISSY. (*Trying to get past Louie Dunbar.*) Watch out, Louie Dunbar! Murray Moskowitz needs me . . . Louie Dunbar! (*Louie Dunbar blocks her exit and Murray Moskowitz crawls back into the tent after one trip around and a strength-seeking deep breath.*)

MURRAY. Okay. I'm all right now.

SISSY. Thank heaven. I tried to come to you but—

LOUIE. Okay, listen! (*Everybody listens—if reluctantly.*) Okay, I been really figurin it out. See, what we do is we wait till after lunch and then we play like we're fixin up a fort—

RICHARD RICHARD. How come a fort?

LOUIE. (*Ignoring Richard Richard.*) Then when this—

RICHARD RICHARD. How come a fort, Louie Dunbar?

LOUIE. Then when this Myron—

SISSY. All right, Louie Dunbar, just because Richard Richard's the youngest Perch doesn't mean you're not gonna have to answer one of his questions. I mean, one day, Louie Dunbar, you're gonna have to answer one of his questions—and I mean it.

LOUIE. *But not today!* God, I'm tryin to—

SISSY. Murray Moskowitz for Commander! (*Sissy Frankel and Murray Moskowitz raise their hands.*)

LOUIE. (*Insistently.*) We make like we're fixin up a fort, see?

Then when this Myron stupenagle comes, I'll talk real tough like we got a secret weapon, ya know? and I'll tell him to get out or somethin or we'll kill 'im. Then I'll say we're makin his gang part of ours and Mur's Assistant Commander and stupe Myron's only a three-star general. (*Louie Dunbar looks to Murray Moskowitz, hopeful of support.*)

MURRAY. Assistant Commander, huh?

BOYSY. I'm a corporal then. (*Boysy dives across the tent onto Richard Richard.*)

MURRAY. Hey, shut it, Boysy, huh! Come on, cut it out, Boysy, you're gonna rip out the tent pegs and then we're really gonna be in for it. (*Boysy is shoved back toward his place. He elbows the assiduously silent Eddie Berkowitz in the chest in passing.*)

SISSY. All right, Louie Dunbar, I just saw Boysy smack Eddie Berkowitz a good one in the gut. You think that doesn't hurt? And where're we gonna be if Eddie's laid up? (*To Eddie.*) You don't say much, do ya, Eddie? But when the chips are down, you're a very tough guy. Correct me if I'm wrong. (*Eddie Berkowitz smiles, punches his fist into his palm. Tough.*)

MURRAY. Look, do ya mind!

SISSY. Are you yelling at *me*, Murray Moskowitz?

MURRAY. All's I'm sayin is let's get on with the plan. Go ahead, Louie Dunbar. So far it's as good as any war plan I ever heard.

LOUIE. So that's it.

MURRAY. That's it?

SISSY. That's it?

LOUIE. Sure. See, he sees he can't beat us and so we move into the foxholes, ya know? and practice and Myron'll take orders from me—

SISSY. Sure he will.

LOUIE. —and do what I say unless I say Mur can tell him somethin; then he'll do that. (*Louie Dunbar scans the Perch. They are dubious, at best. Louie Dunbar begins to nod his head as if he's amazed that anybody was smart enough to figure out such a scheme. Slowly the Perch begin to nod their heads—with the exception of Sissy Frankel who isn't falling for it—nod their heads, trying almost as hard as Louie Dunbar to convince themselves that his plan will work.*) Okay? (*With the exception of Sissy Frankel, the Perch nod big and in unison.*) Okay. Break for lunch. (*Louie Dunbar claps his hands once like a quarterback releasing his team from the huddle and the Perch, except for Louie Dunbar and Sissy Frankel, stampede out of the tent and go galloping back to their original positions on imaginary horses.)*

SISSY. It'll never work, Louie Dunbar.

LOUIE. Wanna bet?

SISSY. No, I do'wanna bet, Louie Dunbar. Whuddo I care? It's your funeral. *(She gallops off to her position. Louie Dunbar slowly, unsurely moves to where Boysy sits miming eating his lunch.)*

LOUIE. I managed about half a salami sandwich for lunch and tried not to watch Boysy pack away two onion sandwiches, a cucumber, three carrots, a raw turnip, but only about ten vanilla wafers because Mom said he'd have diarrhea if he didn't stop. Boysy was like that. He could pack away enormous quantities of lunch, even if I had to make a very tough speech right after. *(The Perch mime the next section, trying gamely to hide their fear.)* After lunch I had the Perch round up about twenty empty cement bags from the bomb shelter Richard Richard's father was building, and I had them fill the bags with grass and pine cones and some garbage from the Dunbar-Moskowitz cans, and stack them around the pup tent like it was a pillbox.

RICHARD RICHARD. *(To Boysy.)* Ya know what I wanna know, Boysy? I'd just like to know how come a fort is all. *(Boysy raps Richard Richard one in the kidneys.)*

LOUIE. Then I had them collect rocks and fix piles so everybody would have easy access to ammo. And then Murray Moskowitz, who I was convinced was only a jerk about ninety percent of his life, brought out his two-gun holster set. *(Murray Moskowitz makes a "showdown at Dodge City" move D. to Louie Dunbar. For a moment, all the Perch are caught up in it.)*

MURRAY. *(Stopping toughly before Louie Dunbar, then breaking.)* I could tell 'em they were real.

SISSY. That's fantastic! Oh—it's brilliant, Murray! Murray Moskowitz for Commander! I demand an immediate vote, Louie Dunbar.

LOUIE. *(To Sissy Frankel.)* Ya know what? It finally comes to me what this whole thing is with you. You're only almost madly in love with Moskowitz—which is not only the most moron-brained thing I ever heard, but maybe the funniest, since Moskowitz only looks like about every lizard I ever saw.

MURRAY. Oh yeah?

SISSY. Well!

LOUIE. Shut up, Frankel!

SISSY. I will not shut up if I don't feel like it.

LOUIE. (*To Murray.*) Listen, Mur, forget the guns, huh? You won't even fool one person.

BOYSY. I'll wear 'em. (*Boysy is standing on Richard Richard's back. His teeshirt is gathered around his neck and his stomach is distended to impressive size. He has an index finger stuck in his bellybutton.*)

LOUIE. Yeah, good. Give the guns to Boysy.

BOYSY. Gimme them guns, Murray Moskowitz.

LOUIE. Hey, but don't take 'em outta the holsters, ya hear?

BOYSY. Uh-uh.

LOUIE. Aw, come on, will ya! Whuddya tryin to do, ruin everything? (*Murray Moskowitz slowly unstraps his irons.*) Come on, Moskowitz, we haven't got all day. You'd think you were givin away your father's lousy 1776 Ford for cryin out loud.

MURRAY. (*Whining.*) It so happens that my mother doesn't feel good today.

SISSY. Oh no! What's wrong? Should I go to her?

LOUIE. *Hold it!* (*The Perch hold it.*) Whudduya think, we're just foolin around here, or what? (*Pause, Louie Dunbar studies the Perch harshly a moment, trying to determine if they think they're just fooling around.*) Okay. Now. When this Myron comes, you guys are all crouched down and lookin straight ahead, see? Like he should think if he makes one false move he'll get stoned or somethin. (*It is obvious by the very forceful way Louie Dunbar is talking that he's scared to death. The Perch don't feel particularly confident either.*) I'm tellin ya, it's gonna work like a charm.

EDDIE BERKOWITZ. Here they come.

SISSY. That Eddie! Boy, I'm telling ya, Murray, he doesn't say much, but when he does say somethin, about half the time it's beautiful. (*And through the audience comes Myron, followed by Herman. The rest of the Louse Drowners can be real or imagined. We can tell by the looks on the Perch faces that Myron is menacing.*)

LOUIE. And there was Myron. He looked to me like maybe the rottenest human I'd ever seen. He didn't wear glasses or anything and he had on a very tight teeshirt with the sleeves shoved back up over one shoulder and a pack of cigarettes rolled up over the other shoulder. One dungaree leg was rolled way up like you did if you took the chain guard off your bike and he wore the good high-top black sneaks, the ones you wore to gym if you were going to play on the indoor court. (*Whispering to the Perch.*) Look straight ahead. (*The Perch take the positions Louie Dunbar outlined above. Louie stands in front of the fort, arms crossed, uncrossed, crossed again, and silently counts twelve Louse Drowners. Myron raises his arms out from his sides and snaps his fingers. Herman imitates the gesture and snaps to "at ease"—as do the other Louse Drowners, if there are any.*)

MYRON. Big Louie?

LOUIE. (*Very friendly, sticking out his hand which Myron ignores.*) Hi there. You going to Nautilus Junior for seventh?

MYRON. (*Growling.*) Yeah!

LOUIE. Hey, great! Maybe we'll be in the same homeroom.

MYRON. Yippe-yo-ha.

LOUIE. Yeah, yippee-yo—

MYRON. (*Unrolling his pack of cigarets.*) Smoke, Big Louie?

LOUIE. Oh . . . uh . . . no. No thanks. What?—Oh yeah, sure! Not you last name, is it?

MYRON. (*Poking a cigaret in his own mouth after Louie Dunbar has taken one.*) Light? (*Myron performs an elaborate match strike and holds it out for Louie Dunbar.*)

LOUIE. Uh . . . no thanks, I'll . . . uhm . . . I'll save it for later. (*Myron holds the match a moment longer before Louie's face, then lights his own cigaret.*)

MYRON. What time ya want that the war should commence, Big Louie?

LOUIE. War? Oh, there's not gonna be any war. See, we're set up mainly—

MYRON. *There's gonna be a war, Big Louie,* otherwise, I wouldn'ta walked alla way down here. Now, whudduyou, crazy . . . or just stupid?

LOUIE. (*Caught off his guard and unable to think of anything snappier.*) You're crazy. (*Myron turns to look at Herman as if to say, Did you hear what he said to me?*)

MYRON. (*To Louie.*) I heard somebody say I'm crazy, Big Louie. Was that you?

LOUIE. (*Wondering for a moment if he was the one who said it.*) Yeah!

MYRON. You wanna do sompin about it?

LOUIE. (*Wondering a moment if he wants to do something about it.*) Yeah!

MYRON. Wanna put me in a insane asylum or sompin?

LOUIE. (*Wondering a moment if he wants to put him in an insane asylum.*) Yeah! (*Myron holds his arms out and advances on Louie Dunbar.*)

MYRON. Okay, Big Louie, here I am. Take me away to the loony bin.

LOUIE. (*Retreating from Myron's advance.*) I'm not takin you anywhere.

MYRON. Oh no? I got the impression that you was in the mood for makin sompin of it.

LOUIE. Makin somethin of what?

MYRON. Of it.

LOUIE. I'm not makin somethin of *nothin*. You wanna make somethin of it, have a nice time.

MYRON. Seems to me you distinctly said you wanted to make sompin of it foist. So what I wanna know is *what* you wanna make of it.

LOUIE. I don't wanna make *nothin* of it. You wanna make somethin of it, then you say. You're the guest. (*Myron stops his advance, drops his cigaret, grinds it out.*)

MYRON. Okay, Big Louie. I say I'm gonna knock your block off.

LOUIE. Oh-ha, I'd like to see you try, boy. I'd just like to see ya try.

MYRON. (*Advancing again.*) Okay, Big Louie, I'm gonna try.

LOUIE. (*Circling in retreat.*) Yeah—well, I'd just like to see ya try it. That'd really be funny, boy. (*Movement freezes. Louie Dunbar turns to the audience. The action picks up off of his narration.*) And then, as Myron crouched into a boxing stance and I prepared to die, Boysy stood between Myron and me, pointing one of Murray Moskowitz' cap guns at Myron's head.

BOYSY. (*Very matter of factly.*) You lay one of your crumb-bum hands on my brother and I'll blow your stupenagle brains out. (*The physical action which follows is done in slow motion.*)

LOUIE. For a moment nobody moved and several hands reached reflexively skyward; but then Myron lowered his guard and laughed. Then he picked Boysy up under the arms and hurled him to the ground where he lay in a heap, looking up at me, waiting while I looked from him to Myron and back to him and didn't do anything. Then he cried and I looked at him, at his dugarees ripped at the knee, which was skinned and starting to bleed. Why'd ya do that, ya schmuck?

MYRON. I felt like it. You gonna do sompin about it?

LOUIE. Just why'd ya do it I wanna know.

MYRON. I *felt* like it I told ya. Whudduya, deaf?

LOUIE. Boysy's crying stopped long enough to force me to look at him, then his face twisted up and he started wailing and he went hobbling into the house.

MYRON. Ya deaf? Hub?

LOUIE. I didn't know what to do. I wanted to punch Myron, wanted to PUNCH him . . . (*Pause.*) . . . but couldn't. I thought . . . I thought: Maybe Boysy'll go in and tell Mom and she'll come out and . . . (*His voice dies; he holds.*)

MYRON. I think Big Louie's *deaf.*

LOUIE. But Boysy hardly ever told Mom anything if something was wrong.

MYRON. (*Screaming in Louie Dunbar's ear.*) Hey, Big Louie, ya there?

LOUIE. (*Raising his fists to Myron.*) I oughta kill you!

MYRON. Yeah, sure. Okay, now you got two choices.

LOUIE. If you hurt him . . .

MYRON. And here they are: You can join my gang or we attack in ten minutes. No—make it fifteen. I gotta go home and get my switchblade.

RICHARD RICHARD. (*Having moved between Louie Dunbar and Myron, to Myron.*) You know how come we built a fort?

MYRON. No—how come, kid?

RICHARD RICHARD. I don't know. I don't know how come.

LOUIE. SHUT UP! THERE'S GOTTA BE SOME SHUTTIN UP AROUND HERE SO'S I CAN THINK!

MYRON. (*Thrusting his arms out.*) Okay—everybody better shut up.

HERMAN. (*Imitating Myron.*) Okay, everybody: Shut up!

MYRON. Take it, Big Louie.

LOUIE. (*Pawing at the ground a moment, trying desperately to "take it", but he can't, so:*) I gotta have a conference.

MYRON. Give ya a minute.

HERMAN. One minute conference! (*Myron begins to silently*

85

tick off the time: "One-one-thousand, two-one-thousand," etc.
Louie Dunbar signals the Perch, who reluctantly make of them-
selves the crammed pup tent. Louie Dunbar is unable to look at any
of the Perch.)

LOUIE. *(Whispering.)* Play like we're joining, okay? Then what
we do is take over from the inside. *(There is no response from any
of the Perch.)* See? *(The Perch don't see.)* Just watch me.

SISSY. I *been* watchin you, Louie Dunbar, and frankly I'm not
too impressed with what I've seen.

LOUIE. *(Forcing himself to play through her remark.)* Just watch
me. I'll let ya know what ya should do. *(The Perch simply stare
at Louie Dunbar, so Louie Dunbar forces some affirmative nodding
and finally creeps out of the tent. The Perch follow slowly.)*

SISSY. *(To Murray Moskowitz, loudly enough for Louie Dunbar
to hear.)* If you'd been Commander, Murray Moskowitz, I guar-
antee that things woulda been a lot different, boy. *(Everybody
freezes a moment, catching Louie Dunbar in his agony. The action
becomes fluid again and Louie Dunbar moves on to Myron.)*

LOUIE. Okay, we're joining.

MYRON. Okay, Prince Herman, line 'em up.

HERMAN. Okay, you new people, line up! *(The Perch line up.
The Perch and Myron and his gang mime the next section.)*

LOUIE. So the war on Tatem opened at two and by two-thirty the
conquered Perch were being marched off to dig foxholes. Which
wasn't such a distasteful thing in itself, but Myron made us dig our
foxholes in the back of the lot, behind his gang's.

MYRON. *(To Herman.)* Dig 'em in the back.

HERMAN. Okay, Louie Dunbar's gang, dig 'em in the back!

LOUIE. And then Herman put a row of dead grass between the
two groups—

HERMAN. Cross this line and you're in trouble.

LOUIE. —and worse yet, for me anyway, Boysy showed up with
iodine on his knee and Myron sort of apologized to him by faking
a left-right combination to the gut and making him a corporal in
the new gang.

MYRON. You're a corporal in the new gang, kid. Whudduya say?

BOYSY. *(Pondering a moment.)* Okay.

HERMAN. Boysy Dunbar's a corporal in the new gang. Let's
hear it!

THE PERCH. (*Without* **real** *enthusiasm.*) Yay, Boysy! (*Boysy crosses to Louie Dunbar and delivers his line—*)

BOYSY. I'm a corporal. (*—then moves off as Louie Dunbar is about to try to say something to him; moves off and elaborately ignores Louie Dunbar.*)

LOUIE. At about three-thirty, when the new diggings were complete and had been given uniform D-minuses by Herman— (*Herman marches past the Perch foxholes and under Louie Dunbar says, "This is a D-minus, this is a D-minus," etc.*) —Myron called everybody together at HQ.

MYRON. HQ, Prince Herman.

HERMAN. Okay, HQ everybody!

RICHARD RICHARD. What's HQ? (*Everybody ignores Richard Richard and moves to where Myron stands on an elevation.*)

HERMAN. (*To Richard Richard.*) Hey, you: HQ! (*Richard Richard follows.*)

MYRON. Okay, everybody in Louie Dunbar's gang is buck privates with the exception of Boysy here, a good man what I'm expectin a lotta good work from, and Louie Dunbar, a former Commander-in-Chief now demoted to a lieutenant. (*Murray Moskowitz and Sissy Frankel take great, if covert, pleasure in Louie Dunbar's huge demotion.*)

LOUIE. (*Toward the audience, but to himself.*) From Commander-in-Chief to a lieutenant? Not even a lousy prince! (*To the audience.*) Hey, I said to Myron, I gotta be better'n a lieutenant. . . . But I must not have said it like I meant it because Myron told me to shut up.

MYRON. Shut up!

LOUIE. And you could tell he meant it by the way his face twisted up. Myron then suggested that each of the new gang members bring him some comic books as an offering.

MYRON. I could use some comics.

LOUIE. Comics for King Myron! That was really something! I could just see bringing him about five top comics and watching him eat jam all over them and then not lending any in return. I was really getting mad. (*To Myron, meekly.*) Do we have to?

MYRON. Ya oughta. We gotta all get closer together, right?

MURRAY. Right!

MYRON. I like Roy Rogers.

MURRAY. I got about eight ya can have.

LOUIE. Oh, that Moskowitz was a marvel. I was really becoming nuts about him.

SISSY. Louie Dunbar's got a ton of 'em. Hand 'em over, Louie Dunbar.

LOUIE. Uh-uh! *Nix!* (*Louie Dunbar's had enough. He shoves his way to where Myron stands.*) I'm not givin you no comics. It's stupid! Why should I give you comics? I think you're a fartface moron faker. (*There is a low rumbling of "ooohs" and "aaahs", there is Louie Dunbar, fists clenched at his sides; and there is Myron.*)

MYRON. I do'wanna hafta kill ya, Louie Dunbar, but—

LOUIE. Kill me! Go ahead! Go ahead—kill me!

MYRON. Okay, Louie, you're a dead Dunbar. But first, for wisin off . . . Moskowitz here is lieutenant. You're lieutenant, Moskowitz.

MURRAY. Hey, thanks, My.

HERMAN. (*Snapping.*) King Myron!

MURRAY. Yeah—King, I mean.

MYRON. Just do your job and keep your people in line.

MURRAY. Gotcha! Okay, my people, keep in line! (*The Perch, wherever they are, make compulsive little moves to keep in line, though without much energy.*)

LOUIE. And Murray Moskowitz looked at me as if I was the only guy in the world who'd never been his best friend. (*This next is mimed by Murray Moskowitz and Louie.*) From this day on, I hardly said five words to Murray Moskowitz, and when the Moskowitzs moved back to Detroit the next year with their goulash, Murray gave me one of his model aiplanes. I stomped it to bits right in front of him without saying a word. Just jumped up and down on it and smashed it to smitherines.

MYRON. You're a buck private, Big Louie. See what happens. (*The fight sequence is danced-fought in slow motion.*)

LOUIE. In my whole life, I'd never really punched anyone. So when I swung at Myron I wasn't surprised that I closed my eyes and hit him in the chest. I also wasn't surprised that Myron stopped threatening to smash me one and smashed me one and that I fell backward and that Myron jumped on me and started pounding me about the head, his knees on my arms, his trunk posting my stomach as if I were a pony. (*The action freezes, Myron's fist raised, about to descend into Louie Dunbar's face. Boysy comes forward as Louie Dunbar narrates it and, in slow motion, delivers the* coup de grace, *a cap gun whack to Myron's nose with one of Murray Moskowitz' guns.*) What did surprise me was that suddenly Myron fell off of me and when I opened my eyes to find out what was going on, I saw Myron bleeding from his nose and there stood Boysy holding one of Murray Moskowitz' cap guns by the muzzle.

MYRON. I'm bleeding. Blood. From my nose.

LOUIE. And Myron started to rise up after Boysy who calmly clonked him a second time. (*Myron starts to cry—*)

HERMAN. King—don't cry! (*—and Louie Dunbar gets to his knees and grabs Boysy—*)

SISSY. Boysy for Commander! (*—and Myron jogs for home, covering his nose and crying.*)

HERMAN. (*Calling after him.*) King!

BOYSY. You okay, Louie Dunbar? (*Louie Dunbar, still on his knees, nods and Boysy pats him on the head, then puts an arm around Louie Dunbar's neck.*)

RICHARD RICHARD. (*To Herman.*) How come foxholes is what I wanna know.

HERMAN. Because. Well, I guess I'm king. Okay—everybody line up! (*But everybody goes home except Louie Dunbar and Herman. The others turn and move u. into the levels and freeze in tableau with their backs to the audience. Finding himself rejected and gangless, Herman follows, leaving Louie Dunbar on his knees. The lights fade but for one on him. He gets to his feet.*)

LOUIE. Little was ever said about that day, but it wasn't until I was a junior in college nine years later, on an afternoon in the spring, during an intramural basketball game, when the ZAE against whom my brother had scored sixteen points, crashed into him from the rear on a breakaway lay-up and sent Boysy skidding across the asphalt, tearing open his knees and elbows, that I raced from the sidelines and, as the ZAE turned to raise his hand to acknowledge the foul that would surely be called, shattered the boy's nose, broke three of my own knuckles, and ended the war on Tatem. (*Louie Dunbar turns u. and holds. Blackout.*)

CURTAIN

PROPERTY LIST

Bag of Barbecue chips (Murray)
Cigarettes and matches (Myron)
Cap pistols (Murray)

NEW PLAYS

★ **YELLOWMAN by Dael Orlandersmith.** A multi-character memory play about an African-American woman who dreams of life beyond the confines of her small-town Southern upbringing and the light-skinned man whose fate is tragically intertwined with hers. Finalist for the Pulitzer Prize. "…prophetic and affirmative…a battle cry for humanity and its possibilities." *–NY Times.* "Both a celebration of young love and a harrowing study of smoldering domestic violence, the play is both heartwarming and ultimately heart-breaking." *–Variety.* [1M, 1W] ISBN: 0-8222-1880-1

★ **THE GUYS by Anne Nelson.** Less than two weeks after the events of September 11th, an editor named Joan comes together with a fire captain to help craft eulogies for firemen lost in the attack. Based on a true story. "Ms. Nelson's play…gives credible and powerful voice to a very specific kind of pain…perhaps the keenest message to emerge from *The Guys* is the assertion that writers—and actors—have a serious role to play in a grieving society." *–NY Times.* [1M, 1W] ISBN: 0-8222-1908-6

★ **HEDWIG AND THE ANGRY INCH by John Cameron Mitchell and Stephen Trask.** The story of "internationally ignored song stylist" Hedwig Schmidt, a fourth-wall smashing East German rock 'n' roll goddess who also happens to be the victim of a botched sex-change operation, which has left her with just "an angry inch." "In the whole long, sorry history of rock musicals, *Hedwig and the Angry Inch* is the first one that truly rocks." *–Rolling Stone.* [1M, 1W (flexible casting)] ISBN: 0-8222-1901-8

★ **BOSTON MARRIAGE by David Mamet.** Set in a drawing room, this droll comedy of errors follows two scheming "women of fashion" as they exchange barbs, taunt their Scottish maid and conspire in pursuit of social and sexual conquests as the Victorian era draws to a close. "Devastatingly funny…exceptionally clever…[Mamet] demonstrates anew his technical virtuosity and flexibility." *–NY Times.* "…[a] marriage of glinting period artifice and contemporary frankness." *–Boston Phoenix.* [3W] ISBN: 0-8222-1944-1

★ **THE LIEUTENANT OF INISHMORE by Martin McDonagh.** On a lonely road on the island of Inishmore, someone killed an IRA enforcer's cat. He'll want to know who when he gets back from a stint of torture and chip-shop bombing in Northern Ireland. He loves his cat more than life itself, and someone is going to pay. "…cunningly constructed, deeply and intensely felt, bitterly blood curdling and breathtakingly funny." *–Sunday Times (London).* "The plot is so sublime, the script so witty and the twist at the end so clever that I was won over…" *–The Stage.* [7M, 1W] ISBN: 0-8222-1934-4

★ **THE DAZZLE by Richard Greenberg.** A pair of early twentieth-century bachelor brothers bury themselves under collectibles and trash in their Harlem mansion in this gorgeous tale of mental collapse. Loosely based on the true story of the Collyer brothers. "…a beautiful, disturbing, shockingly funny and profoundly humane play by a masterful dramatist—a writer fearless in his use of poetic imagery, bitterly acid in his irony and, simultaneously, rapturously romantic and horrifyingly clear eyed in his assessment of life." *–Chicago Sun-Times.* [2M, 1W] ISBN: 0-8222-1915-8

★ **BLUE/ORANGE by Joe Penhall.** In a London psychiatric hospital, an enigmatic patient claims to be the son of an exiled African dictator—a story that becomes unnervingly plausible—in this incendiary tale of race, madness and a Darwinian power struggle at the heart of Britain's deteriorating National Health Service. "Exuberant…Penhall has the gift of making serious points in a comic manner and of conveying moral indignation without preaching." *–Guardian (London).* [3M] ISBN: 0-8222-1935-2

DRAMATISTS PLAY SERVICE, INC.
440 Park Avenue South, New York, NY 10016 212-683-8960 Fax 212-213-1539
postmaster@dramatists.com   www.dramatists.com

NEW PLAYS

★ **SHEL'S SHORTS by Shel Silverstein.** Lauded poet, songwriter and author of children's books, the incomparable Shel Silverstein's short plays are deeply infused with the same wicked sense of humor that made him famous. "...[a] childlike honesty and twisted sense of humor." –*Boston Herald.* "...terse dialogue and an absurdity laced with a tang of dread give [*Shel's Shorts*] more than a trace of Samuel Beckett's comic existentialism." –*Boston Phoenix.* [flexible casting] ISBN: 0-8222-1897-6

★ **AN ADULT EVENING OF SHEL SILVERSTEIN by Shel Silverstein.** Welcome to the darkly comic world of Shel Silverstein, a world where nothing is as it seems and where the most innocent conversation can turn menacing in an instant. These ten imaginative plays vary widely in content, but the style is unmistakable. "...[*An Adult Evening*] shows off Silverstein's virtuosic gift for wordplay...[and] sends the audience out...with a clear appreciation of human nature as perverse and laughable." –*NY Times.* [flexible casting] ISBN: 0-8222-1873-9

★ **WHERE'S MY MONEY? by John Patrick Shanley.** A caustic and sardonic vivisection of the institution of marriage, laced with the author's inimitable razor-sharp wit. "...Shanley's gift for acid-laced one-liners and emotionally tumescent exchanges is certainly potent..." –*Variety.* "...lively, smart, occasionally scary and rich in reverse wisdom." –*NY Times.* [3M, 3W] ISBN: 0-8222-1865-8

★ **A FEW STOUT INDIVIDUALS by John Guare.** A wonderfully screwy comedy-drama that figures Ulysses S. Grant in the throes of writing his memoirs, surrounded by a cast of fantastical characters, including the Emperor and Empress of Japan, the opera star Adelina Patti and Mark Twain. "Guare's smarts, passion and creativity skyrocket to awesome heights..." –*Star Ledger.* "...precisely the kind of good new play that you might call an everyday miracle...every minute of it is fresh and newly alive..." –*Village Voice.* [10M, 3W] ISBN: 0-8222-1907-7

★ **BREATH, BOOM by Kia Corthron.** A look at fourteen years in the life of Prix, a Bronx native, from her ruthless girl-gang leadership at sixteen through her coming to maturity at thirty. "...vivid world, believable and eye-opening, a place worthy of a dramatic visit, where no one would want to live but many have to." –*NY Times.* "...rich with humor, terse vernacular strength and gritty detail..." –*Variety.* [1M, 9W] ISBN: 0-8222-1849-6

★ **THE LATE HENRY MOSS by Sam Shepard.** Two antagonistic brothers, Ray and Earl, are brought together after their father, Henry Moss, is found dead in his seedy New Mexico home in this classic Shepard tale. "...His singular gift has been for building mysteries out of the ordinary ingredients of American family life..." –*NY Times.* "...rich moments ...Shepard finds gold." –*LA Times.* [7M, 1W] ISBN: 0-8222-1858-5

★ **THE CARPETBAGGER'S CHILDREN by Horton Foote.** One family's history spanning from the Civil War to WWII is recounted by three sisters in evocative, intertwining monologues. "...bittersweet music—[a] rhapsody of ambivalence...in its modest, garrulous way...theatrically daring." –*The New Yorker.* [3W] ISBN: 0-8222-1843-7

★ **THE NINA VARIATIONS by Steven Dietz.** In this funny, fierce and heartbreaking homage to *The Seagull*, Dietz puts Chekhov's star-crossed lovers in a room and doesn't let them out. "A perfect little jewel of a play." –*Shepherdstown Chronicle.* "...a delightful revelation of a writer at play; and also an odd, haunting, moving theater piece of lingering beauty." –*Eastside Journal (Seattle).* [1M, 1W (flexible casting)] ISBN: 0-8222-1891-7

DRAMATISTS PLAY SERVICE, INC.
440 Park Avenue South, New York, NY 10016 212-683-8960 Fax 212-213-1539
postmaster@dramatists.com www.dramatists.com

NEW PLAYS

★ **BE AGGRESSIVE by Annie Weisman.** Vista Del Sol is paradise, sandy beaches, avocado-lined streets. But for seventeen-year-old cheerleader Laura, everything changes when her mother is killed in a car crash, and she embarks on a journey to the Spirit Institute of the South where she can learn "cheer" with Bible belt intensity. "...filled with lingual gymnastics...stylized rapid-fire dialogue..." –*Variety*. "...a new, exciting, and unique voice in the American theatre..." –*BackStage West*. [1M, 4W, extras] ISBN: 0-8222-1894-1

★ **FOUR by Christopher Shinn.** Four people struggle desperately to connect in this quiet, sophisticated, moving drama. "...smart, broken-hearted...Mr. Shinn has a precocious and forgiving sense of how power shifts in the game of sexual pursuit...He promises to be a playwright to reckon with..." –*NY Times*. "A voice emerges from an American place. It's got humor, sadness and a fresh and touching rhythm that tell of the loneliness and secrets of life...[a] poetic, haunting play." –*NY Post*. [3M, 1W] ISBN: 0-8222-1850-X

★ **WONDER OF THE WORLD by David Lindsay-Abaire.** A madcap picaresque involving Niagara Falls, a lonely tour-boat captain, a pair of bickering private detectives and a husband's dirty little secret. "Exceedingly whimsical and playfully wicked. Winning and genial. A top-drawer production." –*NY Times*. "Full frontal lunacy is on display. A most assuredly fresh and hilarious tragicomedy of marital discord run amok...absolutely hysterical..." –*Variety*. [3M, 4W (doubling)] ISBN: 0-8222-1863-1

★ **QED by Peter Parnell.** Nobel Prize-winning physicist and all-around genius Richard Feynman holds forth with captivating wit and wisdom in this fascinating biographical play that originally starred Alan Alda. "QED is a seductive mix of science, human affections, moral courage, and comic eccentricity. It reflects on, among other things, death, the absence of God, travel to an unexplored country, the pleasures of drumming, and the need to know and understand." –*NY Magazine*. "Its rhythms correspond to the way that people—even geniuses—approach and avoid highly emotional issues, and it portrays Feynman with affection and awe." –*The New Yorker*. [1M, 1W] ISBN: 0-8222-1924-7

★ **UNWRAP YOUR CANDY by Doug Wright.** Alternately chilling and hilarious, this deliciously macabre collection of four bedtime tales for adults is guaranteed to keep you awake for nights on end. "Engaging and intellectually satisfying...a treat to watch." –*NY Times*. "Fiendishly clever. Mordantly funny and chilling. Doug Wright teases, freezes and zaps us." –*Village Voice*. "Four bite-size plays that bite back." –*Variety*. [flexible casting] ISBN: 0-8222-1871-2

★ **FURTHER THAN THE FURTHEST THING by Zinnie Harris.** On a remote island in the middle of the Atlantic secrets are buried. When the outside world comes calling, the islanders find their world blown apart from the inside as well as beyond. "Harris winningly produces an intimate and poetic, as well as political, family saga." –*Independent (London)*. "Harris' enthralling adventure of a play marks a departure from stale, well-furrowed theatrical terrain." –*Evening Standard (London)*. [3M, 2W] ISBN: 0-8222-1874-7

★ **THE DESIGNATED MOURNER by Wallace Shawn.** The story of three people living in a country where what sort of books people like to read and how they choose to amuse themselves becomes both firmly personal and unexpectedly entangled with questions of survival. "This is a playwright who does not just tell you what it is like to be arrested at night by goons or to fall morally apart and become an aimless yet weirdly contented ghost yourself. He has the originality to make you feel it." –*Times (London)*. "A fascinating play with beautiful passages of writing..." –*Variety*. [2M, 1W] ISBN: 0-8222-1848-8

DRAMATISTS PLAY SERVICE, INC.
440 Park Avenue South, New York, NY 10016 212-683-8960 Fax 212-213-1539
postmaster@dramatists.com www.dramatists.com